R. S. Thomas was born in 1913. He won the Heinemann Award in 1955, the Queen's Gold Medal for poetry in 1964 and the Cholmondeley Award in 1978. He has received three Welsh Arts Council Literature Awards. His auto-biography, *Neb*, was published in Welsh in 1985.

COLLECTED POEMS

1945–1990

R. S. Thomas

PHOENIX  GIANT

A PHOENIX GIANT

First published in Great Britain by J. M. Dent 1993.

This edition published in 1995 by Phoenix,
a division of The Orion Publishing Group,
5 Upper St Martin's Lane, London WC2H 9EA

Reprinted 1996

British Library cataloguing in publication data
is available upon request.

Filmset by Selwood Systems Ltd, Midsomer Norton
Printed and bound in Great Britain by
Butler & Tanner Ltd, Frome and London

ISBN 1 85799 354 3

The author and publisher gratefully acknowledge
the use of poems from *Later Poems* (Macmillan London
Ltd, 1983), *Experimenting With An Amen*
(Macmillan London Ltd, 1986), and
Counterpoint (Bloodaxe Books Ltd, 1990).

Contents

CONTENTS

CONTENTS

ix

Out of the Hills

Dreams clustering thick on his sallow skull,
Dark as curls, he comes, ambling with his cattle
From the starved pastures. He has shaken from off his shoulders
The weight of the sky, and the lash of the wind's sharpness
Is healing already under the medicinal sun.
Clouds of cattle breath, making the air heady,
Remember the summer's sweetness, the wet road runs
Blue as a river before him; the legendary town
Dreams of his coming; under the half-closed lids
Of the indolent shops sleep dawdles, emptying the last
Tankards of darkness, before the officious light
Bundles it up the chimney out of sight.

The shadow of the mountain dwindles; his scaly eye
Sloughs its cold care and glitters. The day is his
To dabble a finger in, and, merry as crickets,
A chorus of coins sings in his tattered pockets.
Shall we follow him down, witness his swift undoing
In the indifferent streets: the sudden disintegration
Of his soul's hardness, traditional discipline
Of flint and frost thawing in ludicrous showers
Of maudlin laughter; the limpid runnels of speech
Sullied and slurred, as the beer-glass chimes the hours?
No, wait for him here. At midnight he will return,
Threading the tunnel that contains the dawn
Of all his fears. Be then his fingerpost
Homeward. The earth is patient; he is not lost.

A Labourer

Who can tell his years, for the winds have stretched
So tight the skin on the bare racks of bone
That his face is smooth, inscrutable as stone?
And when he wades in the brown bilge of earth
Hour by hour, or stoops to pull
The reluctant swedes, who can read the look
In the colourless eyes, as his back comes straight
Like an old tree lightened of the snow's weight?
Is there love there, or hope, or any thought
For the frail form broken beneath his tread,
And the sweet pregnancy that yields his bread?

Cyclamen

They are white moths
With wings
Lifted
Over a dark water
In act to fly,
Yet stayed
By their frail images
In its mahogany depths.

A Peasant

Iago Prytherch his name, though, be it allowed,
Just an ordinary man of the bald Welsh hills,
Who pens a few sheep in a gap of cloud.
Docking mangels, chipping the green skin
From the yellow bones with a half-witted grin
Of satisfaction, or churning the crude earth
To a stiff sea of clouds that glint in the wind –
So are his days spent, his spittled mirth
Rarer than the sun that cracks the cheeks
Of the gaunt sky perhaps once in a week.
And then at night see him fixed in his chair
Motionless, except when he leans to gob in the fire.
There is something frightening in the vacancy of his mind.
His clothes, sour with years of sweat
And animal contact, shock the refined,
But affected, sense with their stark naturalness.
Yet this is your prototype, who, season by season
Against siege of rain and the wind's attrition,
Preserves his stock, an impregnable fortress
Not to be stormed even in death's confusion.
Remember him, then, for he, too, is a winner of wars,
Enduring like a tree under the curious stars.

Country Child

Dropped without joy from the gaunt womb he lies,
Maturing in his place against his parents' ageing;
The slow scene unfolds before his luckless eyes
To the puckered window, where the cold storm's raging
Curtains the world, and the grey curlew cries,
Uttering a grief too sharp for the breast's assuaging.

So the days will drift into months and the months to years,
Moulding his mouth to silence, his hand to the plough;
And the world will grow to a few lean acres of grass,
And an orchard of stars in the night's unscaleable boughs.
But see at the bare field's edge, where he'll surely pass,
An ash tree wantons with sensuous body and smooth,
Provocative limbs to play the whore to his youth,
Till hurled with hot haste into manhood he woos and weds
A wife half wild, half shy of the ancestral bed,
The crumbling house, and the whisperers on the stairs.

The Rising of Glyndwr

Thunder-browed and shaggy-throated
All the men were there,
And the women with the hair
That is the raven's and the rook's despair.

Winds awoke, and vixen-footed
Firelight prowled the glade;
The stars were hooded and the moon afraid
To vex the darkness with her yellow braid.

Then he spoke, and anger kindled
In each brooding eye;
Swords and spears accused the sky,
The woods resounded with a bitter cry.

Beasts gave tongue and barn-owls hooted,
Every branch grew loud
With the menace of that crowd,
That thronged the dark, huge as a thundercloud.

Man and Tree

Study this man; he is older than the tree
That lays its gnarled hand on his meagre shoulder,
And even as wrinkled, for the bladed wind
Ploughs up the surface, as the blood runs colder.
Look at his eyes, that are colourless as rain,
Yet hard and clear, knotted by years of pain.

Look at his locks, that the chill wind has left
With scant reluctance for the sun to bleach.
Notice his mouth and the dry, bird-like tongue,
That flutters and fails at the cracked door of his lips.
Dumb now and sapless? Yet this man can teach,
Even as an oak tree when its leaves are shed,
More in old silence than in youthful song.

Affinity

Consider this man in the field beneath,
Gaitered with mud, lost in his own breath,
Without joy, without sorrow,
Without children, without wife,
Stumbling insensitively from furrow to furrow,
A vague somnambulist; but hold your tears,
For his name also is written in the Book of Life.

Ransack your brainbox, pull out the drawers
That rot in your heart's dust, and what have you to give
To enrich his spirit or the way he lives?
From the standpoint of education or caste or creed
Is there anything to show that your essential need
Is less than his, who has the world for church,
And stands bare-headed in the woods' wide porch
Morning and evening to hear God's choir
Scatter their praises? Don't be taken in
By stinking garments or an aimless grin;
He also is human, and the same small star,
That lights you homeward, has inflamed his mind
With the old hunger, born of his kind.

The Mistress

See how earth claims him as he passes by,
Drawing him reluctant to her ample breast.
But why, when she suckled him, raised him high
In sun and shower, why did she dress
Green sap with sinew, fibre with thigh and thew?
Why has she thrust up through the hollow eye
Her tendril longing for the sky's far blue?
How could she teach him, by intricate weaving
Of wind and air with the frail bones, craving
For flight and freedom, and suddenly sunder
Dreamer from dream in a mute surrender?

Memories of Yeats
Whilst Travelling to Holyhead

How often he went on this journey, think of it, think of it:
The metrical train, the monosyllabic sea,
The listening hilltops, aloof and resentful of strangers.
Who would have refrained from addressing him here, not discerning
The embryonic poem still coiled in the ivory skull?
Boredom or closeness of age might have prompted, his learning
Concealed by his tweed and the azure, ecstatic tie;
But who would have sensed the disdain of his slow reply
Of polite acquiescence in their talk of the beautiful?
Who could have guessed the futility even of praising
Mountain and marsh and the delicate, flickering tree
To one long impervious and cold to the outward scene,
Heedless of nature's baubles, lost in the amazing
And labyrinth paths of his own impenetrable mind?

But something in the hair's fine silver, the breadth of brow,
Had kept me dumb, too shy of his scornful anger
To presume to pierce the dark, inscrutable glasses,
His first defence against a material world.
Yet alone with him in the indifferent compartment, hurled
Between the waves' white audience, the earth's dim screen,
In mutual silence closer than lover knit
I had known reality dwindle, the dream begin.

Country Church

(Manafon)

The church stands, built from the river stone,
Brittle with light, as though a breath could shatter
Its slender frame, or spill the limpid water,
Quiet as sunlight, cupped within the bone.

It stands yet. But though soft flowers break
In delicate waves round limbs the river fashioned
With so smooth care, no friendly God has cautioned
The brimming tides of fescue for its sake.

Peasant Greeting

No speech; the raised hand affirms
All that is left unsaid
By the mute tongue and the unmoistened lips:
The land's patience and a tree's
Knotted endurance and
The heart's doubt whether to curse or bless,
All packed into a single gesture.
The knees crumble to the downward pull
Of the harsh earth, the eyes,
Fuddled with coldness, have no skill to smile.
Life's bitter jest is hollow, mirthless he slips
To his long grave under the wave of wind,
That breaks continually on the brittle ear.

A Priest to His People

Men of the hills, wantoners, men of Wales,
With your sheep and your pigs and your ponies, your sweaty females,
How I have hated you for your irreverence, your scorn even
Of the refinements of art and the mysteries of the Church,
I whose invective would spurt like a flame of fire
To be quenched always in the coldness of your stare.
Men of bone, wrenched from the bitter moorland,
Who have not yet shaken the moss from your savage skulls,
Or prayed the peat from your eyes,
Did you detect like an ewe or an ailing wether,
Driven into the undergrowth by the nagging flies,
My true heart wandering in a wood of lies?

You are curt and graceless, yet your sudden laughter
Is sharp and bright as a whipped pool,
When the wind strikes or the clouds are flying;
And all the devices of church and school
Have failed to cripple your unhallowed movements,
Or put a halter on your wild soul.
You are lean and spare, yet your strength is a mockery
Of the pale words in the black Book,
And why should you come like sparrows for prayer crumbs,
Whose hands can dabble in the world's blood?

I have taxed your ignorance of rhyme and sonnet,
Your want of deference to the painter's skill,
But I know, as I listen, that your speech has in it
The source of all poetry, clear as a rill
Bubbling from your lips; and what brushwork could equal
The artistry of your dwelling on the bare hill?

You will forgive, then, my initial hatred,
My first intolerance of your uncouth ways,
You who are indifferent to all that I can offer,
Caring not whether I blame or praise.
With your pigs and your sheep and your sons
     and holly-cheeked daughters
You will still continue to unwind your days
In a crude tapestry under the jealous heavens
To affront, bewilder, yet compel my gaze.

On a Portrait of
Joseph Hone by Augustus John

As though the brute eyes had seen
In the hushed meadows the weasel,
That would tear the soft down of the throat
And suck the veins dry
Of their glittering blood.

And the mouth formed to the cry,
That gushed from the cleft heart
And flowed coldly as spring water over
The stone lips.

Iago Prytherch

Ah, Iago, my friend, whom the ignorant people thought
The last of your kind, since all the wealth you brought
From the age of gold was the yellow dust on your shoes,
Spilled by the meadow flowers, if you should choose
To wrest your barns from the wind and the weather's claws,
And break the hold of the moss on roof and gable;
If you can till your fields and stand to see
The world go by, a foolish tapestry
Scrawled by the times, and lead your mares to stable,
And dream your dream, and after the earth's laws
Order your life and faith, then you shall be
The first man of the new community.

The Airy Tomb

Twm was a dunce at school, and was whipped and shaken
More than I care to say, but without avail,
For where one man can lead a horse to the pail
Twenty can't make him drink what is not to his mind,
And books and sums were poison to Tomos, he was stone blind
To the print's magic; yet his grass-green eye
Missed nor swoop nor swerve of the hawk's wing
Past the high window, and the breeze could bring,
Above the babble of the room's uproar,
Songs to his ear from the sun-dusted moor,
The grey curlew's whistle and the shrill, far cry
Of circling buzzard ... This was Twm at school,
Subject to nothing but the sky and the wind's rule.
And then at fourteen term ended and the lad was free.
Scatheless as when he entered, he could write and spell
No more than the clouds could or the dribbling rain,
That scrawled vague messages on the window pane.

And so he returned to the Bwlch to help his father
With the rough work of the farm, to ditch, and gather
The slick ewes from the hill; to milk the cow,
And coax the mare that dragged the discordant plough.
Stepping with one stride thus from boy to man,
His school books finished with, he now began
Learning what none could teach but the hill people
In that cold country, where grass and tree
Are a green heritage more rich and rare
Than a queen's emerald or an untouched maid.
It were as well to bring the tup to the wild mare,
Or put the heron and the hen to couple,
As mate a stranger from the fat plain
With that gaunt wilderness, where snow is laid
Deadly as leprosy till the first of May,
And a man counts himself lucky if All Saints' Day
Finds his oats hived in the tottering barn.
But Tomos took to the life like a hillman born;
His work was play after the dull school, and hands,
Shamed by the pen's awkwardness, toyed with the fleece

Of ewe and wether; eyes found a new peace
Tracing the poems, which the rooks wrote in the sky.

So his shadow lengthened, and the years sped by
With the wind's quickness; Twm had turned nineteen,
When his father sickened and at the week's end died,
Leaving him heir to the lean patch of land,
Pinned to the hill-top, and the cloudy acres,
Kept as a sheep-walk. At his mother's side
He stood in the graveyard, where the undertaker
Sprinkled earth rubble with a loud tattoo
On the cheap coffin; but his heart was hurt
By the gash in the ground, and too few, too few
Were the tears that he dropped for that lonely man
Beginning his journey to annihilation.
He had seen sheep rotting in the wind and sun,
And a hawk floating in a bubbling pool,
Its weedy entrails mocking the breast
Laced with bright water; but the dead and living
Moved hand in hand on the mountain crest
In the calm circle of taking and giving.
A wide sepulchre of brisk, blue air
Was the beasts' portion, but a mortal's lot
The boards' strictness, and an ugly scar
On the earth's surface, till the deliberate sod
Sealed off for ever the green land he trod.

But the swift grass, that covered the unsightly wound
In the prim churchyard, healed Tomos' mind
Of its grave-sickness, and December shadows
Dwindled to nothingness in the spring meadows,
That were blowsy with orchis and the loose bog-cotton.
Then the sun strengthened and the hush of June
Settled like lichen on the thick-timbered house,
Where Twm and his mother ate face to face
At the bare table, and each tick of the clock
Was a nail knocked in the lid of the coffin
Of that pale, spent woman, who sat with death
Jogging her elbow through the hot, still days
Of July and August, or passed like a ghost
By the scurrying poultry – it was ever her boast
Not to stay one winter with the goodman cold

In his callous bed. Twm was bumpkin blind
To the vain hysteria of a woman's mind,
And prated of sheep fairs, but the first frost came
To prove how ungarnished was the truth she told.

Can you picture Tomos now in the house alone,
The room silent, and the last mourner gone
Down the hill pathway? Did he sit by the flame
Of his turf fire and watch till dawn
The slow crumbling of the world he had known?
Did he rebuild out of the ragged embers
A new life, tempered to the sting of sorrow?
Twm went to bed and woke on the grey morrow
To the usual jobbery in sty and stable;
Cleaned out the cow-house, harnessed the mare,
And went prospecting with the keen ploughshare.
Yet sometimes the day was dark, and the clouds remembered,
Herded in the bare lanes of sky, the funeral rite,
And Tomos about the house or set at table
Was aware of something for which he had no name,
Though the one tree, which dripped through the winter night
With a clock's constancy, tried hard to tell
The insensitive mind what the heart knew well.

But March squalls, making the windows rattle,
Blew great gaps in his thoughts, till April followed
With a new sweetness, that set the streams gossiping.
On Easter Day he heard the first warbler sing
In the quick ash by the door, and the snow made room
On the sharp turf for the first fumbling lamb.
Docking and grading now until after dark
In the green field or fold, there was too much work
For the mind to wander, though the robin wove
In the young hazel a sweet tale of love.
And what is love to an uncultured youth
In the desolate pastures, but the itch of cattle
At set times and seasons? Twm rarely went down
With his gay neighbours to the petticoat town
In a crook of the valley, and his mind was free
Of the dream pictures which lead to romance.
Hearts and arrows, scribbled at the lane's entrance,
Were a meaningless symbol, as esoteric

As his school fractions; the one language he knew
Was the shrill scream in the dark, the shadow within the shadow,
The glimmer of flesh, deadly as mistletoe.

Of course there was talk in the parish, girls stood at their doors
In November evenings, their glances busy as moths
Round that far window; and some, whom passion made bolder
As the buds opened, lagged in the bottom meadow
And coughed and called. But never a voice replied
From that grim house, nailed to the mountain side,
For Tomos was up with the lambs, or stealthily hoarding
The last light from the sky in his soul's crannies.
So the tongues still wagged, and Tomos became a story
To please a neighbour with, or raise the laughter
In the lewd tavern, for folk cannot abide
The inscrutable riddle, posed by their own kin.
And you, hypocrite reader, at ease in your chair,
Do not mock their conduct, for are you not also weary
Of this odd tale, preferring the usual climax?
He was not well-favoured, you think, nor gay, nor rich,
But surely it happened that one of those supple bitches
With the sly haunches angled him into her net
At the male season, or, what is perhaps more romantic,
Some lily-white maid, a clerk or a minister's daughter,
With delicate hands, and eyes brittle as flowers
Or curved sea-shells, taught him the tender airs
Of a true gallant?
           No, no, you must face the fact
Of his long life alone in that crumbling house
With winds rending the joints, and the grey rain's claws
Sharp in the thatch; of his work up on the moors
With the moon for candle, and the shrill rabble of stars
Crowding his shoulders. For Twm was true to his fate,
That wound solitary as a brook through the crimson heather,
Trodden only by sheep, where youth and age
Met in the circle of a buzzard's flight
Round the blue axle of heaven; and a fortnight gone
Was the shy soul from the festering flesh and bone
When they found him there, entombed in the lucid weather.

Spring Equinox

Do not say, referring to the sun,
'Its journey northward has begun,'
As though it were a bird, annually migrating,
That now returns to build in the rich trees
Its nest of golden grass. Do not belie
Its lusty health with words such as imply
A pallid invalid recuperating.
The age demands the facts, therefore be brief—
Others will sense the simile – and say:
'We are turning towards the sun's indifferent ray.'

The Welsh Hill Country

Too far for you to see
The fluke and the foot-rot and the fat maggot
Gnawing the skin from the small bones,
The sheep are grazing at Bwlch-y-Fedwen,
Arranged romantically in the usual manner
On a bleak background of bald stone.

Too far for you to see
The moss and the mould on the cold chimneys,
The nettles growing through the cracked doors,
The houses stand empty at Nant-yr-Eira,
There are holes in the roofs that are thatched with sunlight,
And the fields are reverting to the bare moor.

Too far, too far to see
The set of his eyes and the slow pthisis
Wasting his frame under the ripped coat,
There's a man still farming at Ty'n-y-Fawnog,
Contributing grimly to the accepted pattern,
The embryo music dead in his throat.

Song for Gwydion

When I was a child and the soft flesh was forming
Quietly as snow on the bare boughs of bone,
My father brought me trout from the green river
From whose chill lips the water song had flown.

Dull grew their eyes, the beautiful, blithe garland
Of stipples faded, as light shocked the brain;
They were the first sweet sacrifice I tasted,
A young god, ignorant of the blood's stain.

Maes-yr-Onnen

Though I describe it stone by stone, the chapel
Left stranded in the hurrying grass,
Painting faithfully the mossed tiles and the tree,
The one listener to the long homily
Of the ministering wind, and the dry, locked doors,
And the stale piety, mouldering within;
You cannot share with me that rarer air,
Blue as a flower and heady with the scent
Of the years past and others yet to be,
That brushed each window and outsoared the clouds'
Far foliage with its own high canopy.
You cannot hear as I, incredulous, heard
Up in the rafters, where the bell should ring,
The wild, sweet singing of Rhiannon's birds.

The Old Language

England, what have you done to make the speech
My fathers used a stranger at my lips,
An offence to the ear, a shackle on the tongue
That would fit new thoughts to an abiding tune?
Answer me now. The workshop where they wrought
Stands idle, and thick dust covers their tools.
The blue metal of streams, the copper and gold
Seams in the wood are all unquarried; the leaves'
Intricate filigree falls, and who shall renew
Its brisk pattern? When spring wakens the hearts
Of the young children to sing, what song shall be theirs?

The Evacuee

She woke up under a loose quilt
Of leaf patterns, woven by the light
At the small window, busy with the boughs
Of a young cherry; but wearily she lay,
Waiting for the syren, slow to trust
Nature's deceptive peace, and then afraid
Of the long silence, she would have crept
Uneasily from the bedroom with its frieze
Of fresh sunlight, had not a cock crowed,
Shattering the surface of that limpid pool
Of stillness, and before the ripples died
One by one in the field's shallows,
The farm awoke with uninhibited din.

And now the noise and not the silence drew her
Down the bare stairs at great speed.
The sounds and voices were a rough sheet
Waiting to catch her, as though she leaped
From a scorched story of the charred past.

And there the table and the gallery
Of farm faces trying to be kind
Beckoned her nearer, and she sat down
Under an awning of salt hams.

And so she grew, a shy bird in the nest
Of welcome that was built about her,
Home now after so long away
In the flowerless streets of the drab town.
The men watched her busy with the hens,
The soft flesh ripening warm as corn
On the sticks of limbs, the grey eyes clear,
Rinsed with dew of their long dread.
The men watched her, and, nodding, smiled
With earth's charity, patient and strong.

The Ancients of the World

The salmon lying in the depths of Llyn Llifon,
    Secretly as a thought in a dark mind,
Is not so old as the owl of Cwm Cowlyd
    Who tells her sorrow nightly on the wind.

The ousel singing in the woods of Cilgwri,
    Tirelessly as a stream over the mossed stones,
Is not so old as the toad of Cors Fochno
    Who feels the cold skin sagging round his bones.

The toad and the ousel and the stag of Rhedynfre,
    That has cropped each leaf from the tree of life,
Are not so old as the owl of Cwm Cowlyd,
    That the proud eagle would have to wife.

Depopulation of the Hills

Leave it, leave it – the hole under the door
Was a mouth through which the rough wind spoke
Ever more sharply; the dank hand
Of age was busy on the walls
Scrawling in blurred characters
Messages of hate and fear.

Leave it, leave it – the cold rain began
At summer end – there is no road
Over the bog, and winter comes
With mud above the axletree.

Leave it, leave it – the rain dripped
Day and night from the patched roof
Sagging beneath its load of sky.

Did the earth help them, time befriend
These last survivors? Did the spring grass
Heal winter's ravages? The grass
Wrecked them in its draughty tides,
Grew from the chimney-stack like smoke,
Burned its way through the weak timbers.
That was nature's jest, the sides
Of the old hulk cracked, but not with mirth.

The Gap in the Hedge

That man, Prytherch, with the torn cap,
I saw him often, framed in the gap
Between two hazels with his sharp eyes,
Bright as thorns, watching the sunrise
Filling the valley with its pale yellow
Light, where the sheep and the lambs went haloed
With grey mist lifting from the dew.
Or was it a likeness that the twigs drew
With bold pencilling upon that bare
Piece of the sky? For he's still there
At early morning, when the light is right
And I look up suddenly at a bird's flight.

Cynddylan on a Tractor

Ah, you should see Cynddylan on a tractor.
Gone the old look that yoked him to the soil;
He's a new man now, part of the machine,
His nerves of metal and his blood oil.
The clutch curses, but the gears obey
His least bidding, and lo, he's away
Out of the farmyard, scattering hens.
Riding to work now as a great man should,
He is the knight at arms breaking the fields'
Mirror of silence, emptying the wood
Of foxes and squirrels and bright jays.
The sun comes over the tall trees
Kindling all the hedges, but not for him
Who runs his engine on a different fuel.
And all the birds are singing, bills wide in vain,
As Cynddylan passes proudly up the lane.

The Hill Farmer Speaks

I am the farmer, stripped of love
And thought and grace by the land's hardness;
But what I am saying over the fields'
Desolate acres, rough with dew,
Is, Listen, listen, I am a man like you.

The wind goes over the hill pastures
Year after year, and the ewes starve,
Milkless, for want of the new grass.
And I starve, too, for something the spring
Can never foster in veins run dry.

The pig is a friend, the cattle's breath
Mingles with mine in the still lanes;
I wear it willingly like a cloak
To shelter me from your curious gaze.

The hens go in and out at the door
From sun to shadow, as stray thoughts pass
Over the floor of my wide skull.
The dirt is under my cracked nails;
The tale of my life is smirched with dung;
The phlegm rattles. But what I am saying
Over the grasses rough with dew
Is, Listen, listen, I am a man like you.

The Tree

Owain Glyn Dŵr Speaks

Gruffudd Llwyd put into my head
The strange thought, singing of the dead
In *awdl* and *cywydd* to the harp,
As though he plucked with each string
The taut fibres of my being.
Accustomed to Iolo and his praise
Of Sycharth with its brown beer,
Meat from the chase, fish from the weir,
Its proud women sipping wine,
I had equated the glib bards
With flattery and the expected phrase,
Tedious concomitants of power.
But Gruffudd Llwyd with his theme
Of old princes in whose veins
Swelled the same blood that sweetened mine
Pierced my lethargy, I heard
Above the tuneful consonants
The sharp anguish, the despair
Of men beyond my smooth domain
Fretting under the barbed sting
Of English law, starving among
The sleek woods no longer theirs.
And I remembered that old nurse
Prating of omens in the sky
When I was born, the heavens inflamed
With meteors and the stars awry.
I shunned the thought, there was the claim
Of wife and young ones, my first care,
And Sycharth, too; I would dismiss
Gruffudd. But something in his song
Stopped me, held me; the bright harp
Was strung with fire, the music burned
All but the one green thought away.
The thought grew to a great tree
In the full spring time of the year;
The far tribes rallied to its green
Banner waving in the wind;
Its roots were nourished with their blood.

And days were fair under those boughs;
The dawn foray, the dusk carouse
Bred the stout limb and blither heart
That marked us of Llywelyn's brood.
It was with us as with the great;
For one brief hour the summer came
To the tree's branches and we heard
In the green shade Rhiannon's birds
Singing tirelessly as the streams
That pluck glad tunes from the grey stones
Of Powys of the broken hills.

The music ceased, the obnoxious wind
And frost of autumn picked the leaves
One by one from the gaunt boughs;
They fell, some in a gold shower
About its roots, but some were hurled
Out of my sight, out of my power,
Over the face of the grim world.

It is winter still in the bare tree
That sprang from the seed which Gruffudd sowed
In my hot brain in the long nights
Of wine and music on the hearth
Of Sycharth of the open gates.
But here at its roots I watch and wait
For the new spring so long delayed;
And he who stands in the light above
And sets his ear to the scarred bole,
Shall hear me tell from the deep tomb
How sorrow may bud the tree with tears,
But only his blood can make it bloom.

Death of a Peasant

You remember Davies? He died, you know,
With his face to the wall, as the manner is
Of the poor peasant in his stone croft
On the Welsh hills. I recall the room
Under the slates, and the smirched snow
Of the wide bed in which he lay,
Lonely as an ewe that is sick to lamb
In the hard weather of mid-March.
I remember also the trapped wind
Tearing the curtains, and the wild light's
Frequent hysteria upon the floor,
The bare floor without a rug
Or mat to soften the loud tread
Of neighbours crossing the uneasy boards
To peer at Davies with gruff words
Of meaningless comfort, before they turned
Heartless away from the stale smell
Of death in league with those dank walls.

The Unborn Daughter

On her unborn in the vast circle
Concentric with our finite lives;
On her unborn, her name uncurling
Like a young fern within the mind;
On her unclothed with flesh or beauty
In the womb's darkness, I bestow
The formal influence of the will,
The wayward influence of the heart,
Weaving upon her fluid bones
The subtle fabric of her being,
Hair, hands and eyes, the body's texture,
Shot with the glory of the soul.

Welsh History

We were a people taut for war; the hills
Were no harder, the thin grass
Clothed them more warmly than the coarse
Shirts our small bones.
We fought, and were always in retreat,
Like snow thawing upon the slopes
Of Mynydd Mawr; and yet the stranger
Never found our ultimate stand
In the thick woods, declaiming verse
To the sharp prompting of the harp.

Our kings died, or they were slain
By the old treachery at the ford.
Our bards perished, driven from the halls
Of nobles by the thorn and bramble.

We were a people bred on legends,
Warming our hands at the red past.
The great were ashamed of our loose rags
Clinging stubbornly to the proud tree
Of blood and birth, our lean bellies
And mud houses were a proof
Of our ineptitude for life.

We were a people wasting ourselves
In fruitless battles for our masters,
In lands to which we had no claim,
With men for whom we felt no hatred.

We were a people, and are so yet.
When we have finished quarrelling for crumbs
Under the table, or gnawing the bones
Of a dead culture, we will arise
And greet each other in a new dawn.

Welsh Landscape

To live in Wales is to be conscious
At dusk of the spilled blood
That went to the making of the wild sky,
Dyeing the immaculate rivers
In all their courses.
It is to be aware,
Above the noisy tractor
And hum of the machine
Of strife in the strung woods,
Vibrant with sped arrows.
You cannot live in the present,
At least not in Wales.
There is the language for instance,
The soft consonants
Strange to the ear.
There are cries in the dark at night
As owls answer the moon,
And thick ambush of shadows,
Hushed at the fields' corners.
There is no present in Wales,
And no future;
There is only the past,
Brittle with relics,
Wind-bitten towers and castles
With sham ghosts;
Mouldering quarries and mines;
And an impotent people,
Sick with inbreeding,
Worrying the carcase of an old song.

Valediction

You failed me, farmer, I was afraid you would
The day I saw you loitering with the cows,
Yourself one of them but for the smile,
Vague as moonlight, cast upon your face
From some dim source, whose nature I mistook.
The hills had grace, the light clothed them
With wild beauty, so that I thought,
Watching the pattern of your slow wake
Through seas of dew, that you yourself
Wore that same beauty by the right of birth.

I know now, many a time since
Hurt by your spite or guile that is more sharp
Than stinging hail and treacherous
As white frost forming after a day
Of smiling warmth, that your uncouthness has
No kinship with the earth, where all is forgiven,
All is requited in the seasonal round
Of sun and rain, healing the year's scars.

Unnatural and inhuman, your wild ways
Are not sanctioned; you are condemned
By man's potential stature. The two things
That could redeem your ignorance, the beauty
And grace that trees and flowers labour to teach,
Were never yours, you shut your heart against them.
You stopped your ears to the soft influence
Of birds, preferring the dull tone
Of the thick blood, the loud, unlovely rattle
Of mucus in the throat, the shallow stream
Of neighbours' trivial talk.
          For this I leave you
Alone in your harsh acres, herding pennies
Into a sock to serve you for a pillow
Through the long night that waits upon your span.

The Labourer

There he goes, tacking against the fields'
Uneasy tides. What have the centuries done
To change him? The same garments, frayed with light
Or seamed with rain, cling to the wind-scoured bones
And shame him in the eyes of the spruce birds.
Once it was ignorance, then need, but now
Habit that drapes him on a bush of cloud
For life to mock at, while the noisy surf
Of people dins far off at the world's rim.
He has been here since life began, a vague
Movement among the roots of the young grass.
Bend down and peer beneath the twigs of hair,
And look into the hard eyes, flecked with care;
What do you see? Notice the twitching hands,
Veined like a leaf, and tough bark of the limbs,
Wrinkled and gnarled, and tell me what you think.
A wild tree still, whose seasons are not yours,
The slow heart beating to the hidden pulse
Of the strong sap, the feet firm in the soil?
No, no, a man like you, but blind with tears
Of sweat to the bright star that draws you on.

An Old Woman

Her days are measured out in pails of water,
Drawn from the pump, while drops of milkless tea,
Brewed in the cup, record the passing hours.
Yet neither tea nor heat of the small fire,
Its few red petals drooping in the grate,
Can stop the ice that forms within her veins,
And knots the blood and clouds the clear, blue eye.
At edge of night she sits in the one chair,
That mocks the frailness of her bones, and stares
Out of the leaded window at the moon,
That amber serpent swallowing an egg;
Footsteps she hears not, and no longer sees
The crop of faces blooming in the hedge
When curious children cluster in the dusk,
Vision being weak and ear-drums stiff with age.
And yet if neighbours call she leans and snatches
The crumbs of gossip from their busy lips,
Sharp as a bird, and now and then she laughs,
A high, shrill, mirthless laugh, half cough, half whistle,
Tuneless and dry as east wind through a thistle.

Farm Child

Look at this village boy, his head is stuffed
With all the nests he knows, his pockets with flowers,
Snail-shells and bits of glass, the fruit of hours
Spent in the fields by thorn and thistle tuft.
Look at his eyes, see the harebell hiding there;
Mark how the sun has freckled his smooth face
Like a finch's egg under that bush of hair
That dares the wind, and in the mixen now
Notice his poise; from such unconscious grace
Earth breeds and beckons to the stubborn plough.

The Minister

Characters
Narrator   The Minister
Davies   Buddug

Narrator
In the hill country at the moor's edge
There is a chapel, religion's outpost
In the untamed land west of the valleys,
The marginal land where flesh meets spirit
Only on Sundays and the days between
Are mortgaged to the grasping soil.

This is the land of green hay
And greener corn, because of the long
Tarrying of winter and the late spring.
This is the land where they burn peat
If there is time for cutting it,
And the weather improves for drying it,
And the cart is not too old for carrying it
And doesn't get stuck in the wet bog.

This is the land where men labour
In silence, and the rusted harrow
Breaks its teeth on the grey stones.
Below, the valleys are an open book,
Bound in sunlight; but the green tale
Told in its pages is not true.

'Beloved, let us love one another,' the words are blown
To pieces by the unchristened wind
In the chapel rafters, and love's text
Is riddled by the inhuman cry
Of buzzards circling above the moor.
Come with me, and we will go
Back through the darkness of the vanished years
To peer inside through the low window
Of the chapel vestry, the bare room
That is sour with books and wet clothes.

They chose their pastors as they chose their horses

For hard work. But the last one died
Sooner than they expected; nothing sinister,
You understand, but just the natural
Breaking of the heart beneath a load
Unfit for horses. 'Ay, he's a good 'un,'
Job Davies had said; and Job was a master
Hand at choosing a nag or a pastor.

And Job was right, but he forgot,
They all forgot that even a pastor
Is a man first and a minister after,
Although he wears the sober armour
Of God, and wields the fiery tongue
Of God, and listens to the voice
Of God, the voice no others listen to;
The voice that is the well-kept secret
Of man, like Santa Claus,
Or where baby came from;
The secret waiting to be told
When we are older and can stand the truth.

O, but God is in the throat of a bird;
Ann heard Him speak, and Pantycelyn.
God is in the sound of the white water
Falling at Cynfal. God is in the flowers
Sprung at the feet of Olwen, and Melangell
Felt His heart beating in the wild hare.
Wales in fact is His peculiar home,
Our fathers knew Him. But where is that voice now?
Is it in the chapel vestry, where Davies is using
The logic of the Smithfield?

Davies
A young 'un we want, someone young
Without a wife. Let him learn
His calling first, and choose after
Among our girls, if he must marry.
There's your girl, Pugh; or yours, Parry;
Ministers' wives they ought to be
With those white hands that are too soft
For lugging muck or pulling a cow's
Tits. But ay, he must be young.

Remember that mare of yours, John?

Too old when you bought her; the old sinner
Had had a taste of the valleys first
And never took to the rough grass
In the top fields. You could do nothing
With her, but let her go her way.
Lucky you sold her. But you can't sell
Ministers, so we must have a care
In choosing. Take my advice,
Pick someone young, and I'll soon show him
How things is managed in the hills here.

Narrator
Did you notice the farm on the hill side
A bit larger than the others, a bit more hay
In the Dutch barn, four cows instead of two?
Prosperity is a sign of divine favour:
Whoever saw the righteous forsaken
Or his seed begging their bread? It even entitles
A chapel deacon to a tame pastor.

There were people here before these,
Measuring truth according to the moor's
Pitiless commentary and the wind's veto.
Out in the moor there is a bone whitening,
Worn smooth by the long dialectic
Of rain and sunlight. What has that to do
With choosing a minister? Nothing, nothing.

Thick darkness is about us, we cannot see
The future, nor the thin face
Of him whom necessity will bring
To this lean oasis at the moor's rim,
The marginal land where flesh meets spirit
Only on Sundays and the days between
Are mortgaged, mortgaged, mortgaged.
But we can see the faces of the men
Grouped together under the one lamp,
Waiting for the name to be born to them
Out of time's heaving thighs.

Did you dream, wanderer in the night,
Of the ruined house with the one light
Shining; and that you were the moth
Drawn relentlessly out of the dark?
The room was empty, but not for long.
You thought you knew them, but they always changed
To something stranger, if you looked closely
Into their faces. And you wished you hadn't come.
You wished you were back in the wide night
Under the stars. But when you got up to go
There was a hand preventing you.
And when you tried to cry out, the cry got stuck
In your dry throat, and you lay there in travail,
Big with your cry, until the dawn delivered you
And your cry was still-born and you arose and buried it,
Laying on it wreaths of the birds' songs.
But for some there is no dawn, only the light
Of the Cross burning up the long aisle
Of night; and for some there is not even that.

The cow goes round and round the field,
Bored with its grass world, and in its eyes
The mute animal hunger, which you pity,
You the confirmed sentimentalist,
Playing the old anthropomorphic game.
But for the cow, it is the same world over the hedge.
No one ever teased her with pictures of flyless meadows,
Where the grass is eternally green
No matter how often the tongue bruises it,
Or the dung soils it.

But with man it is otherwise.
His slow wound deepens with the years,
And knows no healing only the sharp
Distemper of remembered youth.

The Minister
The Reverend Elias Morgan, BA:
I am the name on whom the choice fell.
I came in April, I came young
To the hill chapel, where long hymns were sung
Three times on a Sunday, but rarely between

By a lean-faced people in black clothes,
That smelled of camphor and dried sweat.

It was the time when curlews return
To lay their eggs in the brown heather.
Their piping was the spring's cadenza
After winter's unchanging tune.
But no one heard it, they were too busy
Turning the soil and turning the minister
Over and under with the tongue's blade.

My cheeks were pale and my shoulders bowed
With years of study, but my eyes glowed
With a deep, inner pthisic zeal,
For I was the lamp which the elders chose
To thaw the darkness that had congealed
About the hearts of the hill folk.

I wore a black coat, being fresh from college,
With striped trousers, and, indeed, my knowledge
Would have been complete, had it included
The bare moor, where nature brooded
Over her old, inscrutable secret.
But I didn't even know the names
Of the birds and the flowers by which one gets
A little closer to nature's heart.

Unlike the others my house had a gate
And railings enclosing a tall bush
Of stiff cypress, which the loud thrush
Took as its pulpit early and late.
Its singing troubled my young mind
With strange theories, pagan but sweet,
That made the Book's black letters dance
To a tune John Calvin never heard.
The evening sunlight on the wall
Of my room was a new temptation.
Luther would have thrown his Bible at it.
I closed my eyes, and went on with my sermon.

Narrator
A few flowers bloomed beneath the window,

46

Set there once by a kind hand
In the old days, a woman's gesture
Of love against the childless years.
Morgan pulled them up; they were untidy.
He sprinkled cinders there instead.

Who is this opening and closing the Book
With a bang, and pointing a finger
Before him in accusation?
Who is this leaning from the wide pulpit
In judgment, and filling the chapel
With sound as God fills the sky?
Is that his shadow on the wall behind?
Shout on, Morgan. You'll be nothing tomorrow.

The people were pleased with their new pastor;
Their noses dripped and the blood ran faster
Along their veins, as the hot sparks
Fell from his lips on their dry thoughts:
The whole chapel was soon ablaze.
Except for the elders, and even they were moved
By the holy tumult, but not extremely.
They knew better than that.

It was sex, sex, sex and money, money,
God's mistake and the devil's creation,
That took the mind of the congregation
On long journeys into the hills
Of a strange land, where sin was the honey
Bright as sunlight in death's hive.
They lost the parable and found the story,
And their glands told them they were still alive.
Job looked at Buddug, and she at him
Over the pews, and they knew they'd risk it
Some evening when the moon was low.

Buddug
I know the place, under the hedge
In the top meadow; it was where my mam
Got into trouble, and only the stars
Were witness of the secret act.

47

They say her mother was the same.
Well, why not? It's hard on a girl
In these old hills, where youth is short
And boys are scarce; and the ones we'd marry
Are poor or shy. But Job's got money,
And his wife is old. Don't look at me
Like that, Job; I'm trying to listen
To what the minister says. Your eyes
Scare me, yet my bowels ache
With a strange frenzy. This is what
My mother and her mother felt
For the men who took them under the hedge.

Narrator
The moor pressed its face to the window.
The clock ticked on, the sermon continued.
Out in the fir-tree an owl cried
Derision on a God of love.
But no one noticed, and the voice burned on,
Consuming the preacher to a charred wick.

The Minister
I was good that night, I had the *hwyl*.
We sang the verses of the last hymn
Twice. We might have had a revival
If only the organ had kept in time.
But that was the organist's fault.
I went to my house with the light heart
Of one who had made a neat job
Of pruning the branches on the tree
Of good and evil. Llywarch came with me
As far as the gate. Who was the girl
Who smiled at me as she slipped by?

Narrator
There was cheese for supper and cold bacon,
Or an egg if he liked; all of them given
By Job Davies as part of his pay.
Morgan sat down in his white shirt-sleeves
And cut the bacon in slices the way
His mother used to. He sauced each mouthful
With tasty memories of the day.

Supper over, can you picture him there
Slumped in his chair by the red fire
Listening to the clock's sound, shy as a mouse,
Pattering to and fro in the still house?
The fire voice jars; there is no tune to the song
Of the thin wind at the door, and his nearest neighbour
Being three fields' breadth away, it more often seems
That bed is the shortest path to the friendlier morrow.

But he was not unhappy; there were souls to save;
Souls to be rescued from the encroaching wave
Of sin and evil. Morgan stirred the fire
And drove the shadows back into their corners.

The Minister
I held a *seiat*, but no one came.
It was the wrong time, they said, there were the lambs,
And hay to be cut and peat to carry.
Winter was the time for that.
Winter is the time for easing the heart,
For swapping sins and recalling the days
Of summer when the blood was hot.
Ah, the blurred eye and the cold vein
Of age! 'Come home, come home. All is forgiven.'

I began a Bible class;
But no one came,
Only Mali, who was not right in the head.
She had a passion for me, and dreamed of the day ...
I opened the Bible and expounded the Word
To the flies and spiders, as Francis preached to the birds.

Narrator
Over the moor the round sky
Was ripening, and the sun had spread
Its wings and now was heading south
Over the sea, where Morgan followed.
It was August, the holiday month
For ministers; they walked the smooth
Pavements of Aber and compared their lot
To the white accompaniment of the sea's laughter.

49

The Minister
When I returned, strengthened, to the bare manse
That smelled of mould, someone had broken a window
During my absence and let a bird in.
I found it dead, starved, on the warm sill.
There is always the thin pane of glass set up between us
And our desires.
We stare and stare and stare, until the night comes
And the glass is superfluous.
I went to my cold bed saddened, but the wind in the tree
Outside soothed me with echoes of the sea.

Narrator
Harvest, harvest! The oats that were too weak
To hold their heads up had been cut down
And placed in stooks. There was no nonsense
Plaiting the last sheaf and wasting time
Throwing sickles. That was a fad of Prytherch
Of Nant Carfan; but the bugger was dead.
The men took the corn, the beautiful goddess,
By the long hair and threw her on the ground.

Below in the valleys they were thinking of Christmas;
The fields were all ploughed and the wheat in.
But Davies still hadn't made up his mind
Whom they should ask to the Thanksgiving.

The sea's tan had faded; the old pallor
Was back in Morgan's cheeks. In his long fight
With the bare moor, it was the moor that was winning.
The children came into Sunday School
Before he did, and put muck on his stool.
He stood for the whole lesson, pretending not to notice
The sounds in his desk: a mouse probably
Put there to frighten him. They loved their joke.
Say nothing, say nothing. Morgan was learning
To hold his tongue, the wisdom of the moor.
The pulpit is a kind of block-house
From which to fire the random shot
Of innuendo; but woe betide the man

Who leaves the pulpit for the individual
Assault. He spoke to Davies one day:

Davies
Adultery's a big word, Morgans: where's your proof?
You who never venture from under your roof
Once the night's come; the blinds all down
For fear of the moon's bum rubbing the window.
Take a word from me and keep your nose
In the Black Book, so it won't be tempted
To go sniffing where it's not wanted.
And leave us farmers to look to our own
Business, in case the milk goes sour
From your sharp talk before it's churned
To good butter, if you see what I mean.

Narrator
Did you say something?
Don't be too hard on them, there were people here
Before these and they were no better.
And there'll be people after may be, and they'll be
No better; it is the old earth's way
Of dealing with time's attrition.

Snow on the fields, snow on the heather;
The fox was abroad in the new moon
Barking. And if the snow thawed
And the roads cleared there was an election
Meeting in the vestry next the chapel.
Men came and spoke to them about Wales,
The land they lived in without knowing it,
The land that is reborn at such times.
They mentioned Henry Richard and S.R. – the great names;
And Keir Hardie; the names nobody knew.
It was quite exciting, but in the high marginal land
No names last longer than the wind
And the rain let them on the cold tombstone.
They stood outside afterwards and watched the cars
Of the speakers departing down the long road
To civilisation, and walked home
Arguing confusedly under the stars.

The Minister
Winter was like that; a meeting, a foxhunt,
And the weekly journey to market to unlearn
The lesson of Sunday. The rain never kept them
From the packed town, though it kept them from chapel.

> Drive on, farmer, to market
> With your pigs and your lean cows
> To the town, where the dealers are waiting
> And the girl in the green blouse,
> Fresh as a celandine from the spring meadows,
> Builds like a fabulous tale
> Tower upon tower on the counter
> The brown and the golden ale.

Narrator
A year passed, once more Orion
Unsheathed his sword from its dark scabbard;
And Sirius followed, loud as a bird
Whistling to eastward his bright notes.
The stars are fixed, but the earth journeys
By strange migrations towards the cold
Frosts of autumn from the spring meadows.
And we who see them, where have we been
Since last their splendour inflamed our mind
With huge questions not to be borne?

Morgan was part of the place now; he was beginning
To look back as well as forwards:
Back to the green valleys, forward along the track
That dwindled to nothing in the vast moor.
But life still had its surprises. There was the day
They found old Llywarch dead under the wall
Of the grey sheep-fold, and the sheep all in a ring
Staring, staring at the stiff frame
And the pursed lips from which no whistle came.

The Minister
It was my biggest funeral of all; the hills crawled
With black figures, drawn from remote farms
By death's magnet. 'So sudden. It might have been me.'

And there in the cheap coffin Llywarch was lying,
Taller than you thought, and women were trying
To read through their tears the brass plate.

It might have been Davies! Quickly I brushed
The black thought away; but it came back.
My voice deepened; the people were impressed.
Out in the cold graveyard we sang a hymn,
O fryniau Caersalem; and the Welsh hills looked on
Implacably. It was the old human cry.
But let me be fair, let me be fair.
It was not all like this, even the moor
Has moods of softness when the white hair
Of the bog cotton is a silk bed
For dreams to lie on. There was a day
When young Enid of Gors Fach
Pressed an egg into my hand
Smiling, and her father said:
'Take it, Morgans, to please the child.'
I never heard what they said after,
But went to my bed that night happy for once.
I looked from my top window and saw the moon,
Mellow with age, rising over the moor;
There was something in its bland expression
That softened the moor's harshness, stifled the questions
Struggling to my lips; I made a vow,
As other men in other years have done,
To-morrow would be different. I lay down
And slept quietly. But the morrow woke me
To the ancestral fury of the rain
Spitting and clawing at the pane.
I looked out on a grey world, grey with despair.

Narrator
The rhythm of the seasons: wind and rain,
Dryness and heat, and then the wind again,
Always the wind, and rain that is the sadness
We ascribe to nature, who can feel nothing.
The redwings leave, making way for the swallows;
The swallows depart, the redwings are back once more.
But man remains summer and winter through,
Rooting in vain within his dwindling acre.

53

The Minister
I was the chapel pastor, the abrupt shadow
Staining the neutral fields, troubling the men
Who grew there with my glib, dutiful praise
Of a fool's world; a man ordained for ever
To pick his way along the grass-strewn wall
Dividing tact from truth.

                       I knew it all,
Although I never pried, I knew it all.
I knew why Buddug was away from chapel.
I knew that Pritchard, the *Fron*, watered his milk.
I knew who put the ferret with the fowls
In Pugh's hen-house. I knew and pretended I didn't.
And they knew that I knew and pretended I didn't.
They listened to me preaching the unique gospel
Of love; but our eyes never met. And outside
The blood of God darkened the evening sky.

Narrator
Is there no passion in Wales? There is none
Except in the racked hearts of men like Morgan,
Condemned to wither and starve in the cramped cell
Of thought their fathers made them.
Protestantism – the adroit castrator
Of art; the bitter negation
Of song and dance and the heart's innocent joy –
You have botched our flesh and left us only the soul's
Terrible impotence in a warm world.

Need we go on? In spite of all
His courage Morgan could not avert
His failure, for he chose to fight
With that which yields to nothing human.
He never listened to the hills'
Music calling to the hushed
Music within; but let his mind
Fester with brooding on the sly
Infirmities of the hill people.
The pus conspired with the old
Infection lurking in his breast.

In the chapel acre there is a grave,
And grass contending with the stone
For mastery of the near horizon,
And on the stone words; but never mind them:
Their formal praise is a vain gesture
Against the moor's encroaching tide.
We will listen instead to the wind's text
Blown through the roof, or the thrush's song
In the thick bush that proved him wrong,
Wrong from the start, for nature's truth
Is primary and her changing seasons
Correct out of a vaster reason
The vague errors of the flesh.

Children's Song

We live in our own world,
A world that is too small
For you to stoop and enter
Even on hands and knees,
The adult subterfuge.
And though you probe and pry
With analytic eye,
And eavesdrop all our talk
With an amused look,
You cannot find the centre
Where we dance, where we play,
Where life is still asleep
Under the closed flower,
Under the smooth shell
Of eggs in the cupped nest
That mock the faded blue
Of your remoter heaven.

The Village

Scarcely a street, too few houses
To merit the title; just a way between
The one tavern and the one shop
That leads nowhere and fails at the top
Of the short hill, eaten away
By long erosion of the green tide
Of grass creeping perpetually nearer
This last outpost of time past.

So little happens; the black dog
Cracking his fleas in the hot sun
Is history. Yet the girl who crosses
From door to door moves to a scale
Beyond the bland day's two dimensions.

Stay, then, village, for round you spins
On slow axis a world as vast
And meaningful as any poised
By great Plato's solitary mind.

Lament for Prytherch

When I was young, when I was young!
Were you ever young, Prytherch, a rich farmer:
Cows in the byre, sheep in the pen,
A brown egg under each hen,
The barns oozing corn like honey?
You are old now; time's geometry
Upon your face by which we tell
Your sum of years has with sharp care
Conspired and crossed your brow with grief.
Your heart that is dry as a dead leaf
Undone by frost's cruel chemistry
Clings in vain to the bare bough
Where once in April a bird sang.

Song at the Year's Turning

Shelley dreamed it. Now the dream decays.
The props crumble. The familiar ways
Are stale with tears trodden underfoot.
The heart's flower withers at the root.
Bury it, then, in history's sterile dust.
The slow years shall tame your tawny lust.

Love deceived him; what is there to say
The mind brought you by a better way
To this despair? Lost in the world's wood
You cannot stanch the bright menstrual blood.
The earth sickens; under naked boughs
The frost comes to barb your broken vows.

Is there blessing? Light's peculiar grace
In cold splendour robes this tortured place
For strange marriage. Voices in the wind
Weave a garland where a mortal sinned.
Winter rots you; who is there to blame?
The new grass shall purge you in its flame.

Invasion on the Farm

I am Prytherch. Forgive me. I don't know
What you are talking about; your thoughts flow
Too swiftly for me; I cannot dawdle
Along their banks and fish in their quick stream
With crude fingers. I am alone, exposed
In my own fields with no place to run
From your sharp eyes. I, who a moment back
Paddled in the bright grass, the old farm
Warm as a sack about me, feel the cold
Winds of the world blowing. The patched gate
You left open will never be shut again.

The Poacher

Turning aside, never meeting
In the still lanes, fly infested,
Our frank greeting with quick smile,
You are the wind that set the bramble
Aimlessly clawing the void air.
The fox knows you, the sly weasel
Feels always the steel comb
Of eyes parting like sharp rain
Among the grasses its smooth fur.
No smoke haunting the cold chimney
Over your hearth betrays your dwelling
In blue writing above the trees.
The robed night, your dark familiar,
Covers your movements; the slick sun,
A dawn accomplice, removes your tracks
One by one from the bright dew.

Priest and Peasant

You are ill, Davies, ill in mind;
An old canker, to your kind
Peculiar, has laid waste the brain's
Potential richness in delight
And beauty; and your body grows
Awry like an old thorn for lack
Of the soil's depth; and sickness there
Uncurls slowly its small tongues
Of fungus that shall, thickening, swell
And choke you, while your few leaves
Are green still.
              And so you work
In the wet fields and suffer pain
And loneliness as a tree takes
The night's darkness, the day's rain;
While I watch you, and pray for you,
And so increase my small store
Of credit in the bank of God,
Who sees you suffer and me pray
And touches you with the sun's ray,
That heals not, yet blinds my eyes
And seals my lips as Job's were sealed
Imperiously in the old days.

Pisces

Who said to the trout,
You shall die on Good Friday
To be food for a man
And his pretty lady?

It was I, said God,
Who formed the roses
In the delicate flesh
And the tooth that bruises.

The Return

Coming home was to that:
The white house in the cool grass
Membraned with shadow, the bright stretch
Of stream that was its looking-glass;

And smoke growing above the roof
To a tall tree among whose boughs
The first stars renewed their theme
Of time and death and a man's vows.

A Welshman
to any Tourist

We've nothing vast to offer you, no deserts
Except the waste of thought
Forming from mind erosion;
No canyons where the pterodactyl's wing
Falls like a shadow.
The hills are fine, of course,
Bearded with water to suggest age
And pocked with caverns,
One being Arthur's dormitory;
He and his knights are the bright ore
That seams our history,
But shame has kept them late in bed.

The Last of the Peasantry

What does he know? moving through the fields
And the wood's echoing cloisters
With a beast's gait, hunger in his eyes
Only for what the flat earth supplies;
His wisdom dwindled to a small gift
For handling stock, planting a few seeds
To ripen slowly in the warm breath
Of an old God to whom he never prays.

Moving through the fields, or still at home,
Dwarfed by his shadow on the bright wall,
His face is lit always from without,
The sun by day, the red fire at night;
Within is dark and bare, the grey ash
Is cold now, blow on it as you will.

In a Country Church

To one kneeling down no word came,
Only the wind's song, saddening the lips
Of the grave saints, rigid in glass;
Or the dry whisper of unseen wings,
Bats not angels, in the high roof.

Was he balked by silence? He kneeled long,
And saw love in a dark crown
Of thorns blazing, and a winter tree
Golden with fruit of a man's body.

No Through Road

All in vain. I will cease now
My long absorption with the plough,
With the tame and the wild creatures
And man united with the earth.
I have failed after many seasons
To bring truth to birth,
And nature's simple equations
In the mind's precincts do not apply.

But where to turn? Earth endures
After the passing, necessary shame
Of winter, and the old lie
Of green places beckons me still
From the new world, ugly and evil,
That men pry for in truth's name.

Border Blues

All along the border the winds blow
Eastward from Wales, and the rivers flow
Eastward from Wales with the roads and the railways,
Reversing the path of the old migrations.
And the winds say, It is April, bringing scents
Of dead heroes and dead saints.
But the rivers are surly with brown water
Running amok, and the men to tame them
Are walking the streets of a far town.

Spring is here and the birds are singing;
Spring is here and the bells are ringing
In country churches, but not for a bride.
The sexton breaks the unleavened earth
Over the grave.
          Are there none to marry?
There is still an Olwen teasing a smile
Of bright flowers out of the grass,
Olwen in nylons. Quick, quick,
Marry her someone. But Arthur leers
And turns again to the cramped kitchen
Where the old mother sits with her sons and daughters
At the round table. Ysbaddaden Penkawr's
Cunning was childish measured with hers.

*

I was going up the road and Beuno beside me
Talking in Latin and old Welsh,
When a volley of voices struck us; I turned,
But Beuno had vanished, and in his place
There stood the ladies from the council houses:
Blue eyes and Birmingham yellow
Hair, and the ritual murder of vowels.
Excuse me, I said, I have an appointment
On the high moors; it's the first of May
And I must go the way of my fathers
Despite the loneli – you might say rudeness.

69

Sheep song round me in the strong light;
The ancient traffic of glad birds
Returning to breed in the green sphagnum –
What am I doing up here alone
But paying homage to a bleak, stone   .
Monument to an evicted people?
Go back, go back; from the rough heather
The grouse repels me, and with slow step
I turn to go, but down not back.

*

Eryr Pengwern, penngarn llwyt heno ...
We still come in by the Welsh gate, but it's a long way
To Shrewsbury now from the Welsh border.
There's the train, of course, but I like the 'buses;
We go each Christmas to the pantomime:
It was 'The Babes' this year, all about nature.
On the way back, when we reached the hills –
All black they were with a trimming of stars –
Some of the old ones got sentimental,
Singing Pantycelyn; but we soon drowned them;
It's funny, these new tunes are easy to learn.
We reached home at last, but *diawl!* I was tired.
And to think that my grand-dad walked it each year,
Scythe on shoulder to mow the hay,
And his own waiting when he got back.

*

Mi sydd fachgen ifanc, ffôl,
Yn byw yn ôl fy ffansi.
Riding on a tractor,
Whistling tunes
From the world's dance-halls;
Dreaming of the girl, Ceridwen,
With the red lips,
And red nails.
Coming in late,
Rising early
To flog the carcase
Of the brute earth;
A lad of the 'fifties,
Gay, tough,

I sit, as my fathers have done,
In the back pews on Sundays
And have fun.

*

Going by the long way round the hedges;
Speaking to no one, looking north
At every corner, she comes from the wise man.
Five lengths of yarn from palm to elbow
Wound round the throat, then measured again
Till the yarn shrinks, a cure for jaundice.

Hush, not a word. When we've finished milking
And the stars are quiet, we'll get out the car
And go to Llangurig; the mare's bewitched
Down in the pasture, letting feg
Tarnish the mirror of bright grass.

*

Six drops in a bottle,
And an old rhyme
Scratched on a slate
With stone pencil:
Abracadabra,
Count three, count nine;
Bury it in your neighbour's field
At bed-time.

*

As I was saying, I don't hold with war
Myself, but when you join your unit
Send me some of your brass buttons
And I'll have a shot at the old hare
In the top meadow, for the black cow
Is a pint short each morning now.

Be careful, mind where you're going.
These headlights dazzle, their bright blade
Reaps us a rich harvest of shadow.
But when they have gone, it is darker still,
And the vixen moves under the hill

71

With a new boldness, fretting her lust
To rawness on the unchristened grass.
It's easy to stray from the main road
And find yourself at the old *domen*.
I once heard footsteps in the leaves,
And saw men hiding behind the trunks
Of the trees. I never went there again,
Though that was at night, and the night is different.
The day divides us, but at night
We meet in the inn and warm our hearts
At the red beer with yarn and song;
Despite our speech we are not English,
And our wit is sharp as an axe yet,
Finding the bone beneath the skin
And the soft marrow in the bone.
We are not English ... *Ni bydd diwedd*
Byth ar swn y delyn aur.
Though the strings are broken, and time sets
The barbed wire in their place,
The tune endures; on the cracked screen
Of life our shadows are large still
In history's fierce afterglow.

Temptation of a Poet

The temptation is to go back,
To make tryst with the pale ghost
Of an earlier self, to summon
To the mind's hearth, as I would now,
You, Prytherch, there to renew
The lost poetry of our talk
Over the embers of that world
We built together; not built either,
But found lingering on the farm
As sun lingers about the corn
That in the stackyard makes its own light.

And if I yield and you come
As in the old days with nature's
Lore green on your tongue,
Your coat a sack, pinned at the corners
With the rain's drops, could the talk begin
Where it left off? Have I not been
Too long away? There is a flaw
In your first premise, or else the mind's
Acid sours the soft light
That charmed me.
                    Prytherch, I am undone;
The past calls with the cool smell
Of autumn leaves, but the mind draws
Me onward blind with the world's dust,
Seeking a spring that my heart fumbles.

Evans

Evans? Yes, many a time
I came down his bare flight
Of stairs into the gaunt kitchen
With its wood fire, where crickets sang
Accompaniment to the black kettle's
Whine, and so into the cold
Dark to smother in the thick tide
Of night that drifted about the walls
Of his stark farm on the hill ridge.

It was not the dark filling my eyes
And mouth appalled me; not even the drip
Of rain like blood from the one tree
Weather-tortured. It was the dark
Silting the veins of that sick man
I left stranded upon the vast
And lonely shore of his bleak bed.

On Hearing
a Welshman Speak

And as he speaks time turns,
The swift years revolve
Backwards. There Goronwy comes
Again to his own shore.
Now in a mountain parish
The words leave the Book
To swarm in the honeyed mind
Of Morgan. Glyn Dŵr stands
And sees the flames fall back
Like waves from the charred timbers
Before taking his place
Behind the harp's slack bars
From which the singer called him.
Look, in this resinous church,
As the long prayers are wound
Once more on the priest's tongue,
Dafydd reproves his eyes'
Impetuous falconry
About the kneeling girl.
Stones to the walls fly back,
The gay manors are full
Of music; the poets return
To feed at the royal tables.
Who dreams of failure now
That the oak woods are loud
With the last hurrying feet
Seeking the English plain?

Chapel Deacon

Who put that crease in your soul,
Davies, ready this fine morning
For the staid chapel, where the Book's frown
Sobers the sunlight? Who taught you to pray
And scheme at once, your eyes turning
Skyward, while your swift mind weighs
Your heifer's chances in the next town's
Fair on Thursday? Are your heart's coals
Kindled for God, or is the burning
Of your lean cheeks because you sit
Too near that girl's smouldering gaze?
Tell me, Davies, for the faint breeze
From heaven freshens and I roll in it,
Who taught you your deft poise?

Green Categories

You never heard of Kant, did you, Prytherch?
A strange man! What would he have said
Of your life here, free from the remote
War of antinomies; free also
From mind's uncertainty faced with a world
Of its own making?
                    Here all is sure;
Things exist rooted in the flesh,
Stone, tree and flower. Even while you sleep
In your low room, the dark moor exerts
Its pressure on the timbers. Space and time
Are not the mathematics that your will
Imposes, but a green calendar
Your heart observes; how else could you
Find your way home or know when to die
With the slow patience of the men who raised
This landmark in the moor's deep tides?

His logic would have failed; your mind, too,
Exposed suddenly to the cold wind
Of genius, faltered. Yet at night together
In your small garden, fenced from the wild moor's
Constant aggression, you could have been at one,
Sharing your faith over a star's blue fire.

Age

Farmer, you were young once.
And she was there, waiting, the unique flower
That only you could find in the wild moor
Of your experience.
Gathered, she grew to the warm woman
Your hands had imagined
Fondling soil in the spring fields.

And she was fertile; four strong sons
Stood up like corn in June about you.
But, farmer, did you cherish, tend her
As your own flesh, this dry stalk
Where the past murmurs its sad tune?
Is this the harvest of your blithe sowing?

If you had spared from your long store
Of days lavished upon the land
But one for her where she lay fallow,
Drying, hardening, withering to waste.
But now – too late! You're an old tree,
Your roots groping in her in vain.

The Cat
and the Sea

It is a matter of a black cat
On a bare cliff top in March
Whose eyes anticipate
The gorse petals;

The formal equation of
A domestic purr
With the cold interiors
Of the sea's mirror.

Sailor Poet

His first ship; his last poem;
And between them what turbulent acres
Of sea or land with always the flesh ebbing
In slow waves over the salt bones.

But don't be too hard; so to have written
Even in smoke on such fierce skies,
Or to have brought one poem safely to harbour
From such horizons is not now to be scorned.

The View
from the Window

Like a painting it is set before one,
But less brittle, ageless; these colours
Are renewed daily with variations
Of light and distance that no painter
Achieves or suggests. Then there is movement,
Change, as slowly the cloud bruises
Are healed by sunlight, or snow caps
A black mood; but gold at evening
To cheer the heart. All through history
The great brush has not rested,
Nor the paint dried; yet what eye,
Looking coolly, or, as we now,
Through the tears' lenses, ever saw
This work and it was not finished?

The Country Clergy

I see them working in old rectories
By the sun's light, by candlelight,
Venerable men, their black cloth
A little dusty, a little green
With holy mildew. And yet their skulls,
Ripening over so many prayers,
Toppled into the same grave
With oafs and yokels. They left no books,
Memorial to their lonely thought
In grey parishes; rather they wrote
On men's hearts and in the minds
Of young children sublime words
Too soon forgotten. God in his time
Or out of time will correct this.

Ap Huw's Testament

There are four verses to put down
For the four people in my life,
Father, mother, wife

And the one child. Let me begin
With her of the immaculate brow
My wife; she loves me. I know how.

My mother gave me the breast's milk
Generously, but grew mean after,
Envying me my detached laughter.

My father was a passionate man,
Wrecked after leaving the sea
In her love's shallows. He grieves in me.

What shall I say of my boy,
Tall, fair? He is young yet;
Keep his feet free of the world's net.

Death of a Poet

Laid now on his smooth bed
For the last time, watching dully
Through heavy eyelids the day's colour
Widow the sky, what can he say
Worthy of record, the books all open,
Pens ready, the faces, sad,
Waiting gravely for the tired lips
To move once – what can he say?

His tongue wrestles to force one word
Past the thick phlegm; no speech, no phrases
For the day's news, just the one word 'sorry';
Sorry for the lies, for the long failure
In the poet's war; that he preferred
The easier rhythms of the heart
To the mind's scansion; that now he dies
Intestate, having nothing to leave
But a few songs, cold as stones
In the thin hands that asked for bread.

A Blackbird Singing

It seems wrong that out of this bird,
Black, bold, a suggestion of dark
Places about it, there yet should come
Such rich music, as though the notes'
Ore were changed to a rare metal
At one touch of that bright bill.

You have heard it often, alone at your desk
In a green April, your mind drawn
Away from its work by sweet disturbance
Of the mild evening outside your room.

A slow singer, but loading each phrase
With history's overtones, love, joy
And grief learned by his dark tribe
In other orchards and passed on
Instinctively as they are now,
But fresh always with new tears.

Poetry for Supper

'Listen, now, verse should be as natural
As the small tuber that feeds on muck
And grows slowly from obtuse soil
To the white flower of immortal beauty.'

'Natural, hell! What was it Chaucer
Said once about the long toil
That goes like blood to the poem's making?
Leave it to nature and the verse sprawls,
Limp as bindweed, if it break at all
Life's iron crust. Man, you must sweat
And rhyme your guts taut, if you'd build
Your verse a ladder.'
                              'You speak as though
No sunlight ever surprised the mind
Groping on its cloudy path.'

'Sunlight's a thing that needs a window
Before it enter a dark room.
Windows don't happen.'
                              So two old poets,
Hunched at their beer in the low haze
Of an inn parlour, while the talk ran
Noisily by them, glib with prose.

Iago Prytherch

Iago Prytherch, forgive my naming you.
You are so far in your small fields
From the world's eye, sharpening your blade
On a cloud's edge, no one will tell you
How I made fun of you, or pitied either
Your long soliloquies, crouched at your slow
And patient surgery under the faint
November rays of the sun's lamp.

Made fun of you? That was their graceless
Accusation, because I took
Your rags for theme, because I showed them
Your thought's bareness; science and art,
The mind's furniture, having no chance
To install themselves, because of the great
Draught of nature sweeping the skull.

Fun? Pity? No word can describe
My true feelings. I passed and saw you
Labouring there, your dark figure
Marring the simple geometry
Of the square fields with its gaunt question.
My poems were made in its long shadow
Falling coldly across the page.

Power

Power, farmer? It was always yours.
Not the new physics' terrible threat
To the world's axle, nor the mind's subtler
Manipulation of our debt

To nature; but an old gift
For weathering the slow recoil
Of empires with a tree's patience,
Rooted in the dark soil.

On a Line in Sandburg

'Where did the blood come from?
Before I bit, before I sucked
The red meat, the blood was there
Nourishing sweetly the roots of hair.'

'The blood came from your mother
By way of the long gut-cord;
You were the pain in her side;
You were born on a blood-dark tide.'

'My mother also was young
Once, but her cheeks were red
Even then. From its hidden source
The hot blood ran on its old course.

Where did the blood come from?'

Meet the Family

John One takes his place at the table,
He is the first part of the fable;
His eyes are dry as a dead leaf.
Look on him and learn grief.

John Two stands in the door
Dumb; you have seen that face before
Leaning out of the dark past,
Tortured in thought's bitter blast.

John Three is still outside
Drooling where the daylight died
On the wet stones; his hands are crossed
In mourning for a playmate lost.

John All and his lean wife,
Whose forced complicity gave life
To each loathed foetus, stare from the wall,
Dead not absent. The night falls.

Expatriates

Not British ; certainly
Not English. Welsh
With all the associations,
Black hair and black heart
Under a smooth skin,
Sallow as vellum ; sharp
Of bone and wit that is turned
As a knife against us.
Four centuries now
We have been leaving
The hills and the high moors
For the jewelled pavements
Easing our veins of their dark peat
By slow transfusions.
In the drab streets
That never knew
The cold stream's sibilants
Our tongues are coated with
A dustier speech.
With the year's passing
We have forgotten
The far lakes,
Aled and Eiddwen, whose blue litmus
Alone could detect
The mind's acid.

Absolution

Prytherch, man, can you forgive
From your stone altar on which the light's
Bread is broken at dusk and dawn
One who strafed you with thin scorn
From the cheap gallery of his mind?
It was you who were right the whole time;
Right in this that the day's end
Finds you still in the same field
In which you started, your soul made strong
By the earth's incense, the wind's song.
While I have worn my soul bare
On the world's roads, seeking what lay
Too close for the mind's lenses to see,
And come now with the first stars
Big on my lids westward to find
With the slow lifting up of your hand
No welcome, only forgiveness.

Bread

Hunger was loneliness, betrayed
By the pitiless candour of the stars'
Talk, in an old byre he prayed

Not for food; to pray was to know
Waking from a dark dream to find
The white loaf on the white snow;

Not for warmth, warmth brought the rain's
Blurring of the essential point
Of ice probing his raw pain.

He prayed for love, love that would share
His rags' secret; rising he broke
Like sun crumbling the gold air

The live bread for the starved folk.

Farm Wife

Hers is the clean apron, good for fire
Or lamp to embroider, as we talk slowly
In the long kitchen, while the white dough
Turns to pastry in the great oven,
Sweetly and surely as hay making
In a June meadow; hers are the hands,
Humble with milking, but still now
In her wide lap as though they heard
A quiet music, hers being the voice
That coaxes time back to the shadows
In the room's corners. O, hers is all
This strong body, the safe island
Where men may come, sons and lovers,
Daring the cold seas of her eyes.

Epitaph

The poem in the rock and
The poem in the mind
Are not one.
It was in dying
I tried to make them so.

The Dark Well

They see you as they see you,
A poor farmer with no name,
Ploughing cloudward, sowing the wind
With squalls of gulls at the day's end.
To me you are Prytherch, the man
Who more than all directed my slow
Charity where there was need.

There are two hungers, hunger for bread
And hunger of the uncouth soul
For the light's grace. I have seen both,
And chosen for an indulgent world's
Ear the story of one whose hands
Have bruised themselves on the locked doors
Of life; whose heart, fuller than mine
Of gulped tears, is the dark well
From which to draw, drop after drop,
The terrible poetry of his kind.

To the Farmer

And the wars came and you still practised
Your crude obstetrics with flocks and herds.
You went out early under a dawn sky,
Savage with blood, and turned the patience
Of your deep eyes earthward. The crops grew,
Nursed by your hands, to be mown later
By the hot sickle of flame: no tears
Thawed your bleak face with their salt current.
Instead you waited till the ground was cool,
The enemy gone, and led your cattle
To the black fields, where slow but surely
Green blades were brandished, the old triumph
Of nature over the brief violence
Of man. You will not do so again.

Walter Llywarch

I am, as you know, Walter Llywarch,
Born in Wales of approved parents,
Well goitred, round in the bum,
Sure prey of the slow virus
Bred in quarries of grey rain.

Born in autumn at the right time
For hearing stories from the cracked lips
Of old folk dreaming of summer,
I piled them on to the bare hearth
Of my own fancy to make a blaze
To warm myself, but achieved only
The smoke's acid that brings the smart
Of false tears into the eyes.

Months of fog, months of drizzle;
Thought wrapped in the grey cocoon
Of race, of place, awaiting the sun's
Coming, but when the sun came,
Touching the hills with a hot hand,
Wings were spread only to fly
Round and round in a cramped cage
Or beat in vain at the sky's window.

School in the week, on Sunday chapel:
Tales of a land fairer than this
Were not so tall, for others had proved it
Without the grave's passport, they sent
The fruit home for ourselves to taste.

Walter Llywarch – the words were a name
On a lost letter that never came
For one who waited in the long queue
Of life that wound through a Welsh valley.
I took instead, as others had done
Before, a wife from the back pews
In chapel, rather to share the rain
Of winter evenings, than to intrude
On her pale body; and yet we lay

For warmth together and laughed to hear
Each new child's cry of despair.

The Conductor

Finally at the end of the day,
When the sun was buried and
There was no more to say,

He would lift idly his hand,
And softly the small stars'
Orchestra would begin

Playing over the first bars
Of the night's overture.
He listened with the day's breath

Bated, trying to be sure
That what he heard was at one
With his own score, that nothing,

No casual improvisation
Or sounding of a false chord,
Troubled the deep peace.

It was this way he adored
With a god's ignorance of sin
The self he had composed.

The Parish

There was part of the parish that few knew.
They lived in houses on the main road
To God, as they thought, managing primly
The day's dirt, bottling talk
Of birth and marriage in cold eyes;
Nothing to tell in their spick rooms'
Discipline how with its old violence
Grass raged under the floor.

But you knew it, farmer; your hand
Had felt its power, if not your heart
Its loveliness. Somewhere among
Its green aisles you had watched like me
The sharp tooth tearing its prey,
While a bird sang from a tall tree.

Genealogy

I was the dweller in the long cave
Of darkness, lining it with the forms
Of bulls. My hand matured early,

But turned to violence: I was the man
Watching later at the grim ford,
Armed with resentment; the quick stream

Remembers at sunset the raw crime.
The deed pursued me; I was the king
At the church keyhole, who saw death

Loping towards me. From that hour
I fought for right, with the proud chiefs
Setting my name to the broad treaties.

I marched to Bosworth with the Welsh lords
To victory, but regretted after
The white house at the wood's heart.

I was the stranger in the new town,
Whose purse of tears was soon spent;
I filled it with a solider coin

At the dark sources. I stand now
In the hard light of the brief day
Without roots, but with many branches.

Anniversary

Nineteen years now
Under the same roof
Eating our bread,
Using the same air;
Sighing, if one sighs,
Meeting the other's
Words with a look
That thaws suspicion.

Nineteen years now
Sharing life's table,
And not to be first
To call the meal long
We balance it thoughtfully
On the tip of the tongue,
Careful to maintain
The strict palate.

Nineteen years now
Keeping simple house,
Opening the door
To friend and stranger;
Opening the womb
Softly to let enter
The one child
With his huge hunger.

The Musician

A memory of Kreisler once:
At some recital in this same city,
The seats all taken, I found myself pushed
On to the stage with a few others,
So near that I could see the toil
Of his face muscles, a pulse like a moth
Fluttering under the fine skin
And the indelible veins of his smooth brow.

I could see, too, the twitching of the fingers,
Caught temporarily in art's neurosis,
As we sat there or warmly applauded
This player who so beautifully suffered
For each of us upon his instrument.

So it must have been on Calvary
In the fiercer light of the thorns' halo:
The men standing by and that one figure,
The hands bleeding, the mind bruised but calm,
Making such music as lives still.
And no one daring to interrupt
Because it was himself that he played
And closer than all of them the God listened.

Judgment Day

Yes, that's how I was,
I know that face,
That bony figure
Without grace
Of flesh or limb;
In health happy,
Careless of the claim
Of the world's sick
Or the world's poor;
In pain craven –
Lord, breathe once more
On that sad mirror,
Let me be lost
In mist for ever
Rather than own
Such bleak reflections,
Let me go back
On my two knees
Slowly to undo
The knot of life
That was tied there.

Abersoch

There was that headland, asleep on the sea,
The air full of thunder and the far air
Brittle with lightning; there was that girl
Riding her cycle, hair at half-mast,
And the men smoking, the dinghies at rest
On the calm tide. There were people going
About their business, while the storm grew
Louder and nearer and did not break.

Why do I remember these few things,
That were rumours of life, not life itself
That was being lived fiercely, where the storm raged?
Was it just that the girl smiled,
Though not at me, and the men smoking
Had the look of those who have come safely home?

Ninetieth Birthday

You go up the long track
That will take a car, but is best walked
On slow foot, noting the lichen
That writes history on the page
Of the grey rock. Trees are about you
At first, but yield to the green bracken,
The nightjar's house: you can hear it spin
On warm evenings; it is still now
In the noonday heat, only the lesser
Voices sound, blue-fly and gnat
And the stream's whisper. As the road climbs,
You will pause for breath and the far sea's
Signal will flash, till you turn again
To the steep track, buttressed with cloud.

And there at the top that old woman,
Born almost a century back
In that stone farm, awaits your coming;
Waits for the news of the lost village
She thinks she knows, a place that exists
In her memory only.
                    You bring her greeting
And praise for having lasted so long
With time's knife shaving the bone.
Yet no bridge joins her own
World with yours, all you can do
Is lean kindly across the abyss
To hear words that were once wise.

Too Late

I would have spared you this, Prytherch;
You were like a child to me.
I would have seen you poor and in rags,
Rather than wealthy and not free.

The rain and wind are hard masters;
I have known you wince under their lash.
But there was comfort for you at the day's end
Dreaming over the warm ash

Of a turf fire on a hill farm,
Contented with your accustomed ration
Of bread and bacon, and drawing your strength
From membership of an old nation

Not given to beg. But look at yourself
Now, a servant hired to flog
The life out of the slow soil,
Or come obediently as a dog

To the pound's whistle. Can't you see
Behind the smile on the times' face
The cold brain of the machine
That will destroy you and your race?

Hireling

Cars pass him by; he'll never own one.
Men won't believe in him for this.
Let them come into the hills
And meet him wandering a road,
Fenced with rain, as I have now;
The wind feathering his hair;
The sky's ruins, gutted with fire
Of the late sun, smouldering still.

Nothing is his, neither the land
Nor the land's flocks. Hired to live
On hills too lonely, sharing his hearth
With cats and hens, he has lost all
Property but the grey ice
Of a face splintered by life's stone.

Poet's Address
to the
Businessmen

Gentlemen all
At the last crumbfall,
The set of glasses,
The moist eye,
I rise to speak
Of things irrelevant:
The poem shut,
Uneasy fossil,
In the mind's rock;
The growth of winter
In the thick wood
Of history; music
We might have heard
In the heart's cloisters.
I speak of wounds
Not dealt us; blows
That left no bruises
On the white table
Cloth. Forgive me
The tongue's failure,
In all this leanness
Of time, to arrive
Nearer the bone.

Those Others

A gofid gwerin gyfan
Yn fy nghri fel taerni tân.
                    Dewi Emrys

I have looked long at this land,
Trying to understand
My place in it – why,
With each fertile country
So free of its room,
This was the cramped womb
At last took me in
From the void of unbeing.

Hate takes a long time
To grow in, and mine
Has increased from birth;
Not for the brute earth
That is strong here and clean
And plain in its meaning
As none of the books are
That tell but of the war

Of heart with head, leaving
The wild birds to sing
The best songs; I find
This hate's for my own kind,
For men of the Welsh race
Who brood with dark face
Over their thin navel
To learn what to sell;

Yet not for them all either,
There are still those other
Castaways on a sea
Of grass, who call to me,
Clinging to their doomed farms;
Their hearts though rough are warm
And firm, and their slow wake
Through time bleeds for our sake.

Portrait

You never asked what he was like,
That man, Prytherch. Did you class him
With other labourers, breaking the wild
Mare of the soil with bare knuckles
And gnarled thighs, knowing him shut
In cold arenas between hedges
With no audience, a man for whom
The stars' bridle was hung too high?

He was in rags; you were right there.
But the blood was fanned by the sharp draught
Of winter into a huge blaze
In the cheeks' grate, and eyes that you might
Have fancied brown from their long gazing
Downward were of a hard blue,
So shrill they would not permit the ear
To hear what the lips' slobber intended.

Hyddgen

The place, Hyddgen;
The time, the fifth
Century since Glyn Dŵr
Was here with his men.
He beat the English.
Does it matter now
In the rain? The English
Don't want to come:
Summer country.
The Welsh too:
A barren victory.
Look at those sheep,
On such small bones
The best mutton,
But not for him,
The hireling shepherd.
History goes on;
On the rock the lichen
Records it: no mention
Of them, of us.

Lore

Job Davies, eighty-five
Winters old, and still alive
After the slow poison
And treachery of the seasons.

Miserable? Kick my arse!
It needs more than the rain's hearse,
Wind-drawn, to pull me off
The great perch of my laugh.

What's living but courage?
Paunch full of hot porridge,
Nerves strengthened with tea,
Peat-black, dawn found me

Mowing where the grass grew,
Bearded with golden dew.
Rhythm of the long scythe
Kept this tall frame lithe.

What to do? Stay green.
Never mind the machine,
Whose fuel is human souls.
Live large, man, and dream small.

Mother and Son

At nine o'clock in the morning
My son said to me:
Mother, he said, from the wet streets
The clouds are removed and the sun walks
Without shoes on the warm pavements.
There are girls biddable at the corners
With teeth cleaner than your white plates;
The sharp clatter of your dishes
Is less pleasant to me than their laughter.
The day is building; before its bright walls
Fall in dust, let me go
Beyond the front garden without you
To find glasses unstained by tears,
To find mirrors that do not reproach
My smooth face; to hear above the town's
Din life roaring in the veins.

Pharisee.
Twentieth Century

Lord, I was not as most men.
When they were working, fighting, drinking,
I was in the greenwood, thinking
Thought to the bone. Down through my pen
The heart's poetry like blood ran.
When some were in their cars, swanking,
I was on my two knees, thanking
For such grace as I had then.

They felt so, too. Many the jests
From hale lungs and deep chests,
From broad bodies too well to care.
My long face, my long hair
Took them in ; smugly they laughed,
Souls guttering in the grave's draught.

A Welsh Testament

All right, I was Welsh. Does it matter?
I spoke the tongue that was passed on
To me in the place I happened to be,
A place huddled between grey walls
Of cloud for at least half the year.
My word for heaven was not yours.
The word for hell had a sharp edge
Put on it by the hand of the wind
Honing, honing with a shrill sound
Day and night. Nothing that Glyn Dŵr
Knew was armour against the rain's
Missiles. What was descent from him?

Even God had a Welsh name:
We spoke to him in the old language;
He was to have a peculiar care
For the Welsh people. History showed us
He was too big to be nailed to the wall
Of a stone chapel, yet still we crammed him
Between the boards of a black book.

Yet men sought us despite this.
My high cheek-bones, my length of skull
Drew them as to a rare portrait
By a dead master. I saw them stare
From their long cars, as I passed knee-deep
In ewes and wethers. I saw them stand
By the thorn hedges, watching me string
The far flocks on a shrill whistle.
And always there was their eyes' strong
Pressure on me: You are Welsh, they said;
Speak to us so; keep your fields free
Of the smell of petrol, the loud roar
Of hot tractors; we must have peace
And quietness.
                    Is a museum
Peace? I asked. Am I the keeper
Of the heart's relics, blowing the dust
In my own eyes? I am a man;

117

I never wanted the drab rôle
Life assigned me, an actor playing
To the past's audience upon a stage
Of earth and stone; the absurd label
Of birth, of race hanging askew
About my shoulders. I was in prison
Until you came; your voice was a key
Turning in the enormous lock
Of hopelessness. Did the door open
To let me out or yourselves in?

Which?

And Prytherch – was he a real man,
Rolling his pain day after day
Up life's hill? Was he a survival
Of a lost past, wearing the times'
Shabbier casts-off, refusing to change
His lean horse for the quick tractor?
Or was a wish to have him so
Responsible for his frayed shape?

Could I have said he was the scholar
Of the fields' pages he turned more slowly
Season by season, or nature's fool,
Born to blur with his moist eye
The clear passages of a book
You came to finger with deft touch?

Here

I am a man now.
Pass your hand over my brow,
You can feel the place where the brains grow.

I am like a tree,
From my top boughs I can see
The footprints that led up to me.

There is blood in my veins
That has run clear of the stain
Contracted in so many loins.

Why, then, are my hands red
With the blood of so many dead?
Is this where I was misled?

Why are my hands this way
That they will not do as I say?
Does no God hear when I pray?

I have nowhere to go.
The swift satellites show
The clock of my whole being is slow.

It is too late to start
For destinations not of the heart.
I must stay here with my hurt.

Alpine

About mountains it is useless to argue,
You have either been up or you haven't;

The view from half-way is nobody's view.
The best flowers are mostly at the top

Under a ledge, nourished by wind.
A sense of smell is of less importance

Than a sense of balance, walking on clouds
Through holes in which you can see the earth

Like a rich man through the eye of a needle.
The mind has its own level to find.

The Maker

So he said then : I will make the poem,
I will make it now. He took pencil,
The mind's cartridge, and blank paper,
And drilled his thoughts to the slow beat

Of the blood's drum ; and there it formed
On the white surface and went marching
Onward through time, while the spent cities
And dry hearts smoked in its wake.

A Line from St David's

I am sending you this letter,
Something for neo-Edwardians
Of a test-tube age to grow glum about
In their conditioned libraries.
As I came here by way of Plwmp,
There were hawkweeds in the hedges;
Nature had invested all her gold
In the industry of the soil.
There were larks, too, like a fresh chorus
Of dew, and I thought, remembering Dewi
The water-drinker, the way back
Is not so far as the way forward.
Here the cathedral's bubble of stone
Is still unpricked by the mind's needle,
And the wall lettuce in the crevices
Is as green now as when Giraldus
Altered the colour of his thought
By drinking from the Welsh fountain ...

I ramble; what I wanted to say
Was that the day has a blue lining
Partly of sky, partly of sea;
That the old currents are in the grass,
Though rust has becalmed the plough.
Somewhere a man sharpens a scythe;
A child watches him from the brink
Of his own speech, and this is of more
Importance than all the visitors keeping
A spry saint asleep in his tomb.

Country Cures

There are places, where you might have been sent
To learn patience, to make your soul
In long hours by the poor light
Of a few, pale leaves on a tree
In autumn or a flower in spring;
Lost parishes, where the grass keeps
No register and life is bare
Of all but the cold fact of the wind.

I know those places and the lean men,
Whose collars fasten them by the neck
To loneliness; as I go by,
I hear them pacing from room to room
Of their gaunt houses; or see their white
Faces setting on a blank day.

Funeral

They stand about conversing
In dark clumps, less beautiful than trees.
What have they come here to mourn?
There was a death, yes; but death's brother,
Sin, is of more importance.
Shabbily the teeth gleam,
Sharpening themselves on reputations
That were firm once. On the cheap coffin
The earth falls more cleanly than tears.
What are these red faces for?
This incidence of pious catarrh
At the grave's edge? He has returned
Where he belongs; this is acknowledged
By all but the lonely few
Making amends for the heart's coldness
He had from them, grudging a little
The simple splendour of the wreath
Of words the church lays on him.

To a Young Poet

For the first twenty years you are still growing,
Bodily that is; as a poet, of course,
You are not born yet. It's the next ten
You cut your teeth on to emerge smirking
For your brash courtship of the muse.
You will take seriously those first affairs
With young poems, but no attachments
Formed then but come to shame you,
When love has changed to a grave service
Of a cold queen.
          From forty on
You learn from the sharp cuts and jags
Of poems that have come to pieces
In your crude hands how to assemble
With more skill the arbitrary parts
Of ode or sonnet, while time fosters
A new impulse to conceal your wounds
From her and from a bold public,
Given to pry.
          You are old now
As years reckon, but in that slower
World of the poet you are just coming
To sad manhood, knowing the smile
On her proud face is not for you.

Sorry

Dear parents,
I forgive you my life,
Begotten in a drab town,
The intention was good;
Passing the street now,
I see still the remains of sunlight.

It was not the bone buckled;
You gave me enough food
To renew myself.
It was the mind's weight
Kept me bent, as I grew tall.

It was not your fault.
What should have gone on,
Arrow aimed from a tried bow
At a tried target, has turned back,
Wounding itself
With questions you had not asked.

Becoming

Not for long.
After the dark
The dawning.
After the first light
The sun.
After the calm the wind,
Creasing the water.
After the silence
Sound,
Sound of the wild birds,
And movement,
The fox and the hare.
And all these at one,
Part of the tearless content
Of the eye's lens.

But over the sunlight
Shadow
Of the first man.

Welsh

Why must I write so?
I'm Welsh, see:
A real Cymro,
Peat in my veins.
I was born late;
She claimed me,
Brought me up nice,
No hardship;
Only the one loss,
I can't speak my own
Language – Iesu,
All those good words;
And I outside them,
Picking up alms
From blonde strangers.
I don't like their talk,
Their split vowels;
Names that are ghosts
From a green era.
I want my own
Speech, to be made
Free of its terms.
I want the right word
For the gut's trouble,
When I see this land
With its farms empty
Of folk, and the stone
Manuscripts blurring
In wind and rain.
I want the town even,
The open door
Framing a slut,
So she can speak Welsh
And bear children
To accuse the womb
That bore me.

Afforestation

It's a population of trees
Colonising the old
Haunts of men; I prefer,
Listening to their talk,
The bare language of grass
To what the woods say,
Standing in black crowds
Under the stars at night
Or in the sun's way.
The grass feeds the sheep;
The sheep give the wool
For warm clothing, but these –?
I see the cheap times
Against which they grow:
Thin houses for dupes,
Pages of pale trash,
A world that has gone sour
With spruce. Cut them down,
They won't take the weight
Of any of the strong bodies
For which the wind sighs.

The Survivors

I never told you this.
He told me about it often:
Seven days in an open boat – burned out,
No time to get food:
Biscuits and water and the unwanted sun,
With only the oars' wing-beats for motion,
Labouring heavily towards land
That existed on a remembered chart,
Never on the horizon
Seven miles from the boat's bow.

After two days song dried on their lips;
After four days speech.
On the fifth cracks began to appear
In the faces' masks; salt scorched them.
They began to think about death,
Each man to himself, feeding it
On what the rest could not conceal.
The sea was as empty as the sky,
A vast disc under a dome
Of the same vastness, perilously blue.

But on the sixth day towards evening
A bird passed. No one slept that night;
The boat had become an ear
Straining for the desired thunder
Of the wrecked waves. It was dawn when it came,
Ominous as the big guns
Of enemy shores. The men cheered it.
From the swell's rise one of them saw the ruins
Of all that sea, where a lean horseman
Rode towards them and with a rope
Galloped them up on to the curt sand.

The Garden

It is a gesture against the wild,
The ungovernable sea of grass;
A place to remember love in,
To be lonely for a while;
To forget the voices of children
Calling from a locked room;
To substitute for the care
Of one querulous human
Hundreds of dumb needs.

It is the old kingdom of man.
Answering to their names,
Out of the soil the buds come,
The silent detonations
Of power wielded without sin.

Tramp

A knock at the door
And he stands there,
A tramp with his can
Asking for tea,
Strong for a poor man
On his way – where?

He looks at his feet,
I look at the sky;
Over us the planes build
The shifting rafters
Of that new world
We have sworn by.

I sleep in my bed,
He sleeps in the old,
Dead leaves of a ditch.
My dreams are haunted;
Are his dreams rich?
If I wake early,
He wakes cold.

Welcome

You can come in.
You can come a long way;
We can't stop you.
You can come up the roads
Or by railway;
You can land from the air.
You can walk this country
From end to end;
But you won't be inside;
You must stop at the bar,
The old bar of speech.

We have learnt your own
Language, but don't
Let it take you in;
It's not what you mean,
It's what you pay with
Everywhere you go,
Pleased at the price
In shop windows.
There is no way there;
Past town and factory
You must travel back
To the cold bud of water
In the hard rock.

Wallace Stevens

1

On New Year's night after a party
His father lay down and made him
In the flesh of a girl out of Holland.
The baby was dropped at the first fall
Of the leaf, wanting the safe bough
He came from, and was for years dumb,
Mumbling the dry crust
Of poetry, until the teeth grew,
Ivory of a strange piano.

Yet it was not those that he played.
They were too white; he preferred black,
The deep spaces between stars,
Fathomless as the cold shadow
His mind cast. In the bleak autumn
Of real time here I remember
Without eloquence his birth.

2

How like him to bleed at last
Inwardly, but to the death,
Who all his life from the white page
Infected us chiefly with fear
Of the veins' dryness. Words he shed
Were dry leaves of a dry mind,
Crackling as the wind blew
From mortuaries of the cold heart.

There was no spring in his world.
His one season was late fall;
The self ripe, but without taste.
Yet painfully on the poem's crutch
He limped on, taking despair
As a new antidote for love.

Parent

So he took her – just like that,
In a moment of sunlight;
Her haired breast heaving against his,
Her voice fierce;
Her yellow teeth bared for the love bite.

And the warm day indifferent,
Not foreseeing the loading
Of that huge womb;
The seven against Thebes, the many
Against Troy, the whole earth
A confusion of persons,
Each with his grudge
Rooted in the enormous loins
Of the first parent.

A Country

At fifty he was still trying to deceive
Himself. He went out at night,
Imagining the dark country
Between the border and the coast
Was still Wales; the old language
Came to him on the wind's lips;
There were intimations of farms
Whose calendar was a green hill.

And yet under such skies the land
Had no more right to its name
Than a corpse had; self-given wounds
Wasted it. It lay like a bone
Thrown aside and of no use
For anything except shame to gnaw.

A Lecturer

A little man,
Sallow,
Keeping close to the wall
Of life; his quick smile
Of recognition a cure
For loneliness; he'll take you
Any time on a tour
Of the Welsh language, its flowering
While yours was clay soil.

It seeds in him.
Fitfully,
As the mood blows, poetry
In this small plot
Of manhood opens
Its rich petals; the smell
Is familiar. Watch him,
As with short steps he goes.
Not dangerous?
He has been in gaol.

Strangers

We don't like your white cottage.
We don't like the way you live.
Their sins are venial, the folk
With green blouses you displace.
They have gone proudly away,
Leaving only the dry bed
Of footsteps where there was grass,
Or memory of a face
For ever setting within the glass
Of windows about the door.

You have not been here before.
You will offend with your speech
Winds that preferred hands
Wrung with despair, profound
Audiences of the dead.

The Untamed

My garden is the wild
  Sea of the grass. Her garden
Shelters between walls.
  The tide could break in;
  I should be sorry for this.

There is peace there of a kind,
  Though not the deep peace
Of wild places. Her care
  For green life has enabled
  The weak things to grow.

Despite my first love,
  I take sometimes her hand,
Following strait paths
  Between flowers, the nostril
  Clogged with their thick scent.

The old softness of lawns
  Persuading the slow foot
Leads to defection; the silence
  Holds with its gloved hand
  The wild hawk of the mind.

But not for long, windows,
  Opening in the trees
Call the mind back
  To its true eyrie; I stoop
  Here only in play.

Movement

Move with the times?
I've done that all right:
In a few years
Buried a nation.
Words for the sweet tooth
Have gone sour.
Looking at them now,
None of those farms
In the high hills
Have bred children.
My poems were of old men;
The chimney corner
Is a poor place to sing
Reedy accompaniment
To the wheels' rattle,
As life puts on speed.

The Boy's Tale

Skipper wouldn't pay him off,
Never married her;
Came home by Port Said
To a Welsh valley;
Took a girl from the tip,
Sheer coal dust
The blue in her veins.
Every time I go now
Through black sunlight,
I see her scratch his name
On the pane of her breath.
Caught him in her thin hair,
Couldn't hold him –
Voices from the ports
Of the stars, pavilions
Of unstable water.
She went fishing in him;
I was the bait
That became cargo,
Shortening his trips,
Waiting on the bone's wharf.
Her tongue ruled the tides.

Truth

He was in the fields, when I set out.
He was in the fields, when I came back.
In between, what long hours,
What centuries might have elapsed.
Did he look up? His arm half
Lifted was more to ward off
My foolishness. You will return,
He intimated; the heart's roots
Are here under this black soil
I labour at. A change of wind
Can bring the smooth town to a stop;
The grass whispers beneath the flags;
Every right word on your tongue
Has a green taste. It is the mind
Calling you, eager to paint
Its distances; but the truth's here,
Closer than the world will confess,
In this bare bone of life that I pick.

The Mill

I am going back now
Twenty years at least:
Hardly his wife's place
In bed was cold, than
He was there instead
And would not be moved.
It seemed hard at first,
Those who had waited
For years on the one
Now had the other
Lying log heavy
And stiff in that room,
That smelled of death
Or mildew or both.

They just carried on;
Washed him and changed him,
He was one more beast
To be fed and watered
On that hill farm.
Why did they do it?
Was the meagre price
Such bones can command
In death's market
Worth all their trouble?
Had a seed of love,
Left from the threshing,
Found a crack in their hearts?

I called of an evening,
Watched how the lamp
Explored the contours
Of his face's map.
On the wall his shadow
Grew stern as he talked
Of the old exploits
With the plough and scythe.
I read him the psalms,
Said prayers and was still.

In the long silence
I heard in the drawers
The mice that rustled;
In the shallow grate
The small fire's petals
Withered and fell.

Nine years in that bed
From season to season
The great frame rotted,
While the past's slow stream,
Flowing through his head,
Kept the rusty mill
Of the mind turning –
It was I it ground.

Servant

You served me well, Prytherch.
From all my questionings and doubts;
From brief acceptance of the times'
Deities; from ache of the mind
Or body's tyranny, I turned,
Often after a whole year,
Often twice in the same day,
To where you read in the slow book
Of the farm, turning the fields' pages
So patiently, never tired
Of the land's story; not just believing,
But proving in your bone and your blood
Its accuracy; willing to stand
Always aside from the main road,
Where life's flashier illustrations
Were marginal.
                Not that you gave
The whole answer. Is truth so bare,
So dark, so dumb, as on your hearth
And in your company I found it?
Is not the evolving print of the sky
To be read, too; the mineral
Of the mind worked? Is not truth choice,
With a clear eye and a free hand,
From life's bounty?
                  Not choice for you,
But seed sown upon the thin
Soil of a heart, not rich, nor fertile,
Yet capable of the one crop,
Which is the bread of truth that I break.

Souillac:
Le Sacrifice d'Abraham

And he grasps him by the hair
With innocent savagery.
And the son's face is calm;
There is trust there.

And the beast looks on.

This is what art could do,
Interpreting faith
With serene chisel.
The resistant stone
Is quiet as our breath,
And is accepted.

The Figure

He was far out from the shore
Of his four hedges, marooned there
On the bare island of himself.
I watched him from the main road
Over the currents of a sea
Shallow enough for me to cross,
Had I the time, the will – what was it
Kept me? It could have been a part
Of the strange calling I followed,
Wading closer to have found
The dark wrack of his thoughts lifting
And falling round the thick skull;
To have known the colour of his eyes,
Their mitigation of his parched
And waste presence.
                    Were there questions
My lips hardly would have dared
To frame, put there by his own
Brutally at the cold bar
Of reason, where he was arraigned?

On the Farm

There was Dai Puw. He was no good.
They put him in the fields to dock swedes,
And took the knife from him, when he came home
At late evening with a grin
Like the slash of a knife on his face.

There was Llew Puw, and he was no good.
Every evening after the ploughing
With the big tractor he would sit in his chair,
And stare into the tangled fire garden,
Opening his slow lips like a snail.

There was Huw Puw, too. What shall I say?
I have heard him whistling in the hedges
On and on, as though winter
Would never again leave those fields,
And all the trees were deformed.

And lastly there was the girl:
Beauty under some spell of the beast.
Her pale face was the lantern
By which they read in life's dark book
The shrill sentence: God is love.

The Patriot

He had that rare gift that what he said,
Even the simplest statement, could inflame
The mind and heart of the hearer. Those, who saw
For the first time that small figure
With the Welsh words leaving his lips
As quietly as doves on an errand
Of peace-making, could not imagine
The fierceness of their huge entry
At the ear's porch.
                And when he wrote,
Drawing the ink from his own veins'
Blood and iron, the sentences
Opened again the concealed wounds
Of history in the comfortable flesh.

Looking at Sheep

Yes, I know. They are like primroses;
Their ears are the colour of the stems
Of primroses; and their eyes –
Two halves of a nut.
                              But images
Like this are for sheer fancy
To play with. Seeing how Wales fares
Now, I will attend rather
To things as they are: to green grass
That is not ours; to visitors
Buying us up. Thousands of mouths
Are emptying their waste speech
About us, and an Elsan culture
Threatens us.
                              What would they say
Who bled here, warriors
Of a free people? Savagely
On castles they were the sole cause
Of the sun still goes down red.

Rhodri

Rhodri Theophilus Owen,
Nothing Welsh but the name;
He moves in a landscape of dust
That is sourer than the smell
Of breweries. What are the moors
To him? Shadows of boredom
In the mind's corners. He has six shirts
For the week-end and a pocketful
Of notes. Don't mention roots
To Rhodri; his address
Is greater than the population
Of Dolfor, many times
Greater, and in that house
There are three Owens, none with a taste
For the homeland with its pints
Of rain water.
              It is dry
Here, with the hard, dry
Urban heat, that is sickly
With girls. But Rhodri is cool;
From the shadow of his tree
Of manhood he watches them
Pass, or selects one
To make real the power of the pounds,
That in Wales would have gone rather
To patch up the family stocking,
Emblem of a nation's despair.

Because

I praise you because
I envy your ability to
See these things: the blind hands
Of the aged combing sunlight
For pity; the starved fox and
The obese pet; the way the world
Digests itself and the thin flame
Scours. The youth enters
The brothel, and the girl enters
The nunnery, and a bell tolls.
Viruses invade the blood.
On the smudged empires the dust
Lies and in the libraries
Of the poets. The flowers wither
On love's grave. This is what
Life is, and on it your eye
Sets tearless, and the dark
Is dear to you as the light.

Swifts

The swifts winnow the air.
It is pleasant at the end of the day
To watch them. I have shut the mind
On fools. The 'phone's frenzy
Is over. There is only the swifts'
Restlessness in the sky
And their shrill squealing.
                     Sometimes they glide,
Or rip the silk of the wind
In passing. Unseen ribbons
Are trailing upon the air.
There is no solving the problem
They pose, that had millions of years
Behind it, when the first thinker
Looked at them.
                  Sometimes they meet
In the high air; what is engendered
At contact? I am learning to bring
Only my wonder to the contemplation
Of the geometry of their dark wings.

Rose Cottage

Rose Cottage, because it had
Roses. If all things were as
Simple! There was the place
With some score or so of
Houses, all of them red
Brick, with their names clear
To read; and this one, its gate
Mossed over, its roof rusty
With lichen. You chose it out
For its roses, and were not wrong.
It was registered in the heart
Of a nation, and so, sure
Of its being. All summer
It generated the warmth
Of its blooms, red lamps
To guide you. And if you came
Too late in the bleak cold
Of winter, there were the faces
At the window, English faces
With red cheeks, countering the thorns.

Hafod Lom

Hafod Lom, the poor holding:
I have become used to its
Beauty, the ornamentation
Of its bare walls with grey
And gold lichen; to its chimney
Tasselled with grasses. Outside
In the ruined orchard the leaves
Are richer than fruit; music
From a solitary robin plays
Like a small fountain. It is hard
To recall here the drabness
Of past lives, who wore their days
Raggedly, seeking meaning
In a lean rib. Imagine a child's
Upbringing, who took for truth
That rough acreage the rain
Fenced; who sowed his dreams
Hopelessly in the wind blowing
Off bare plates. Yet often from such
Those men came, who, through windows
In the thick mist peering down
To the low country, saw learning
Ready to reap. Their long gnawing
At life's crust gave them teeth
And a strong jaw and perseverance
For the mastication of the fact.

This To Do

I have this that I must do
One day: overdraw on my balance
Of air, and breaking the surface
Of water go down into the green
Darkness to search for the door
To myself in dumbness and blindness
And uproar of scared blood
At the eardrums. There are no signposts
There but bones of the dead
Conger, no light but the pale
Phosphorous, where the slow corpses
Swag. I must go down with the poor
Purse of my body and buy courage,
Paying for it with the coins of my breath.

Within Sound of the Sea

I have a desire to walk on the shore,
To visit the caged beast whose murmurings
Kept me awake. What does it mean
That I have the power to do this
All day long, if I wish to?
I know what thoughts will arise,
What questions. They have done so before,
Unanswered. It is in the freedom
To go or not to I exist;
To balance all the exhilaration
Of brisk moments upon the sand
With the knowledgeable hours that my books
Give me. Between their pages
The beast sleeps and never looks out
Through the print's bars. Have I been wise
In the past, letting my nostrils
Plan my day? That salt scrubbing
Left me unclean. Am I wise now,
With all this pain in the air,
To keep my room, reading perhaps
Of that Being whose will is our peace?

Pietà

Always the same hills
Crowd the horizon,
Remote witnesses
Of the still scene.

And in the foreground
The tall Cross,
Sombre, untenanted,
Aches for the Body
That is back in the cradle
Of a maid's arms.

Amen

And God said: How do you know?
And I went out into the fields
At morning and it was true.

Nothing denied it, neither the bowed man
On his knees, nor the animals,
Nor the birds notched on the sky's

Surface. His heart was broken
Far back, and the beasts yawned
Their boredom. Under the song

Of the larks, I heard the wheels turn
Rustily. But the scene held;
The cold landscape returned my stare;

There was no answer. Accept; accept.
And under the green capitals,
The molecules and the blood's virus.

Gifts

From my father my strong heart,
My weak stomach.
From my mother the fear.

From my sad country the shame.

To my wife all I have
Saving only the love
That is not mine to give.

To my one son the hunger.

Kierkegaard

And beyond the window Denmark
Waited, but refused to adopt
This family that wore itself out
On its conscience, up and down
In the one room.
                    Meanwhile the acres
Of the imagination grew
Unhindered, though always they paused
At that labourer, the indictment
Of whose gesture was a warped
Crucifix upon a hill
In Jutland. The stern father
Looked at it and a hard tear
Formed, that the child's frightened
Sympathy could not convert
To a plaything.
                He lived on,
Søren, with the deed's terrible lightning
About him, as though a bone
Had broken in the adored body
Of his God. The streets emptied
Of their people but for a girl
Already beginning to feel
The iron in her answering his magnet's
Pull. Her hair was to be
The moonlight towards which he leaned
From darkness. The husband stared
Through life's bars, venturing a hand
To pluck her from the shrill fire
Of his genius. The press sharpened
Its rapier; wounded, he crawled
To the monastery of his chaste thought
To offer up his crumpled amen.

For Instance

She gave me good food;
I accepted;

Sewed my clothes, buttons;
I was smart.

She warmed my bed;
Out of it my son stepped.

She was adjudged
Beautiful. I had grown

Used to it. She is dead
Now. Is it true

I loved her? That is how
I saw things. But not she.

For the Record

What was your war record, Prytherch?
I know: up and down the same field,
Following a horse; no oil for tractors;
Sniped at by rain, but never starving.
Did you listen to the reports
Of how heroes are fashioned and how killed?
Did you wait up late for the news?
Your world was the same world as before
Wars were contested, noisier only
Because of the echoes in the sky.
The blast worried your hair on its way to the hill;
The distances were a wound
Opened each night. Yet in your acres,
With no medals to be won,
You were on the old side of life,
Helping it in through the dark door
Of earth and beast, quietly repairing
The rents of history with your hands.

A Welshman
at St James' Park

I am invited to enter these gardens
As one of the public, and to conduct myself
In accordance with the regulations;
To keep off the grass and sample flowers
Without touching them; to admire birds
That have been seduced from wildness by
Bread they are pelted with.
                        I am not one
Of the public; I have come a long way
To realise it. Under the sun's
Feathers are the sinews of stone,
The curved claws.
                        I think of a Welsh hill
That is without fencing, and the men,
Bosworth blind, who left the heather
And the high pastures of the heart. I fumble
In the pocket's emptiness; my ticket
Was in two pieces. I kept half.

The Moor

It was like a church to me.
I entered it on soft foot,
Breath held like a cap in the hand.
It was quiet.
What God was there made himself felt,
Not listened to, in clean colours
That brought a moistening of the eye,
In movement of the wind over grass.

There were no prayers said. But stillness
Of the heart's passions – that was praise
Enough; and the mind's cession
Of its kingdom. I walked on,
Simple and poor, while the air crumbled
And broke on me generously as bread.

There

They are those that life happens to.
They didn't ask to be born
In those bleak farmsteads, but neither
Did they ask not. Life took the seed
And broadcast it upon the poor,
Rush-stricken soil, an experiment
In patience.
                    What is a man's
Price? For promises of a break
In the clouds; for harvests that are not all
Wasted; for one animal born
Healthy, where seven have died,
He will kneel down and give thanks
In a chapel whose stones are wrenched
From the moorland.
                         I have watched them bent
For hours over their trade,
Speechless, and have held my tongue
From its question. It was not my part
To show them, like a meddler from the town,
Their picture, nor the audiences
That look at them in pity or pride.

The Belfry

I have seen it standing up grey,
Gaunt, as though no sunlight
Could ever thaw out the music
Of its great bell; terrible
In its own way, for religion
Is like that. There are times
When a black frost is upon
One's whole being, and the heart
In its bone belfry hangs and is dumb.

But who is to know? Always,
Even in winter in the cold
Of a stone church, on his knees
Someone is praying, whose prayers fall
Steadily through the hard spell
Of weather that is between God
And himself. Perhaps they are warm rain
That brings the sun and afterwards flowers
On the raw graves and throbbing of bells.

Aside

Take heart, Prytherch.
Over you the planets stand,
And have seen more ills than yours.
This canker was in the bone
Before man bent to his image
In the pool's glass. Violence has been
And will be again. Between better
And worse is no bad place

For a labourer, whose lot is to seem
Stationary in traffic so fast.
Turn aside, I said; do not turn back.
There is no forward and no back
In the fields, only the year's two
Solstices, and patience between.

The Visit

She was small;
Composed in her way
Like music. She sat
In the chair I had not
Offered, smiling at my left
Shoulder. I waited on
For the sentences her smile
Sugared.
        That the tongue
Is a whip needed no
Proving. And yet her eye
Fondled me. It was clear
What anger brought her
To my door would not unleash
The coils. Instead she began
Rehearsing for her
Departure. As though ashamed
Of a long stay, she rose,
Touched the tips of my cold
Hand with hers and turned
To the closed door. I remember
Not opening it.

Exchange

She goes out.
I stay in.
Now we have been
So long together
There's no need
To share silence;
The old bed
Remains made
For two; spirits
Mate apart
From the sad flesh,
Growing thinner
On time's diet
Of bile and gall.

Gospel Truth

MARK PUW : Who put me here?
I must get on with this job;
The rain is coming. I must get on
With this job. Who put me
Here? The bugger; I'd like
To see him now in my place.

MATTHEW PUW : There are times
When I could wreck the whole bloody
Farm. Pig music, sheep music, the grey
Traffic of the clouds going by
I could get shut of the lot,
If it wasn't for him and Mair.

LUKE PUW : Every morning I wake,
There is the spilled light in my room;
I rise and try to wash my hands
In its cold water. Then inside
The tune starts; the rest leave me
To play it over to myself.

MAIR PUW : There are the clothes
To wash Mondays, and the plates
To be kept filled; boots to clean.
I have stopped trying to think
What I should do, if that face
In the half-darkness should go out.

MATTHEW PUW : Heaven and heaven's foundations
Rot. I have seen the girl,
Whose flesh is like the warm milk
In pails I have carried these ten years
Without tasting. I am thirsty
As the hard earth in spring and as dry.

MARK PUW : I shall get all the blame
For this. Who put the seed down
In such places? I never wanted
The ground ploughed; better to have left
it

172

As earth wanted it to be,
Fertile of stone, the wind's pasture.

LUKE PUW : Leaves of the sun
Are falling; it is always autumn
Where I go. On bare branches
I look into the eyes of the dumb
Blackbirds. What I sing
Frightens them; it is called 'Luke Puw'.

MAIR PUW : I have watched them come
In from the fields more times than I wish
To be told. My heart is the clapper
Of an old bell, stiff and rusty.
How long will those hands pull
On the rope fastening it to care?

MATTHEW PUW : Under the talk
I am listening to the dusk's
Sounds; the owl and badger
Waken. But that familiar
Drooling has not begun yet
To drill the nerve. Is this it?

MARK PUW : There is an empty
Place at the table; instead
Of a respite from that tune
In the skull, I must endure
The accusation of dead eyes
From a portrait. It is not my fault.

MAIR PUW : This has happened
Before. If I bring myself
To stay still, they will go out
Like dogs that round up a strayed
Sheep. But that inaudible
Whistle – from whose lips does it come?

173

Service

We stand looking at
Each other. I take the word 'prayer'
And present it to them. I wait idly,
Wondering what their lips will
Make of it. But they hand back
Such presents. I am left alone
With no echoes to the amen
I dreamed of. I am saved by music
From the emptiness of this place
Of despair. As the melody rises
From nothing, their mouths take up the tune,
And the roof listens. I call on God
In the after silence, and my shadow
Wrestles with him upon a wall
Of plaster, that has all the nation's
Hardness in it. They see me thrown
Without movement of their oblique eyes.

Blondes

They pass me with bland looks.
It is the simplicity of their lives
I ache for: prettiness and a soft heart, no problems
Not to be brought to life size
By a kiss or a smile. I see them walking
Up long streets with the accuracy of shuttles
At work, threads crossed to make a pattern
Unknown to them. A thousand curtains
Are parted to welcome home
The husbands who have overdrawn
On their blank trust, giving them children
To play with, a jingle of small change
For their pangs. The tear-laden tree
Of a poet strikes no roots in their hearts.

The Dance

She is young. Have I the right
Even to name her? Child,
It is not love I offer
Your quick limbs, your eyes;
Only the barren homage
Of an old man whom time
Crucifies. Take my hand
A moment in the dance,
Ignoring its sly pressure,
The dry rut of age,
And lead me under the boughs
Of innocence. Let me smell
My youth again in your hair.

Who?

Someone must have thought of putting me here;
It wasn't myself did it.
What do I find to my taste?
Annually the grass comes up green;
The earth keeps its rotary motion.
There is loveliness growing, where might have been truth's
Bitterer berries. The reason tempers
Most of the heart's stormier moods.

But there's an underlying despair
Of what should be most certain in my life:
This hard image that is reflected
In mirrors and in the eyes of my friends.
It is for this that the air comes in thin
At the nostril, and dries to a crust.

The Face

When I close my eyes, I can see it,
That bare hill with the man ploughing,
Corrugating that brown roof
Under a hard sky. Under him is the farm,
Anchored in its grass harbour;
And below that the valley
Sheltering its few folk,
With the school and the inn and the church,
The beginning, middle and end
Of their slow journey above ground.

He is never absent, but like a slave
Answers to the mind's bidding,
Endlessly ploughing, as though autumn
Were the one season he knew.
Sometimes he pauses to look down
To the grey farmhouse, but no signals
Cheer him; there is no applause
For his long wrestling with the angel
Of no name. I can see his eye
That expects nothing, that has the rain's
Colourlessness. His hands are broken
But not his spirit. He is like bark
Weathering on the tree of his kind.

He will go on; that much is certain.
Beneath him tenancies of the fields
Will change; machinery turn
All to noise. But on the walls
Of the mind's gallery that face
With the hills framing it will hang
Unglorified, but stern like the soil.

Schoonermen

Great in this,
They made small ships do
Big things, leaping hurdles
Of the stiff sea, horse against horses
In the tide race.
                        What has Rio
To do with Pwllheli? Ask winds
Bitter for ever
With their black shag. Ask the quays
Stained with spittle.
                            Four days out
With bad cargo
Fever took the crew;
The mate and boatswain,
Peering in turn
Through the spray's window,
Brought her home. Memory aches
In the bones' rigging. If tales were tall,
Waves were taller.
                         From long years
In a salt school, caned by brine,
They came landward
With the eyes of boys,
The Welsh accent
Thick in their sails.

In Church

Often I try
To analyse the quality
Of its silences. Is this where God hides
From my searching? I have stopped to listen,
After the few people have gone,
To the air recomposing itself
For vigil. It has waited like this
Since the stones grouped themselves about it.
These are the hard ribs
Of a body that our prayers have failed
To animate. Shadows advance
From their corners to take possession
Of places the light held
For an hour. The bats resume
Their business. The uneasiness of the pews
Ceases. There is no other sound
In the darkness but the sound of a man
Breathing, testing his faith
On emptiness, nailing his questions
One by one to an untenanted cross.

Careers

Fifty-two years,
most of them taken in
growing or in the
illusion of it – what does the mem-
ory number as one's
property? The broken elbow?
the lost toy? The pain has
vanished, but the soft flesh
that suffered it is mine still.

There is a house with
a face mooning at the glass
of windows. Those eyes – I look
at not with them, but something of
their melancholy I
begin to lay claim to as my own.

A boy in school:
his lessons are
my lessons, his
punishments I learn to deserve.
I stand up in him,
tall as I am
now, but without per-
spective. Distant objects
are too distant, yet will arrive
soon. How his words
muddle me; how my deeds
betray him. That is not
our intention; but where I should
be one with him, I am one now
with another. Before I had time
to complete myself, I let her share
in the building. This that I am
now – too many
labourers. What is mine is
not mine only: her love, her
child wait for my slow
signature. Son, from the mirror

you hold to me I turn
to recriminate. That likeness
you are at work upon – it hurts.

A Grave Unvisited

There are places where I have not been;
Deliberately not, like Søren's grave
In Copenhagen. Seeing the streets
With their tedious reproduction
Of all streets, I preferred Dragort,
The cobbled village with its flowers
And pantiles by the clear edge
Of the Baltic, that extinct sea.

What they could do to anchor him
With the heaviness of a nation's
Respectability they have done,
I am sure. I imagine the size
Of his tombstone, the solid marble
Cracking his bones; but would he have been
There to receive this toiling body's
Pilgrimage a few months back,
Had I made it?
           What is it drives a people
To the rejection of a great
Spirit, and after to think it returns
Reconciled to the shroud
Prepared for it? It is Luke's gospel
Warns us of the danger
Of scavenging among the dead
For the living – so I go
Up and down with him in his books,
Hand and hand like a child
With its father, pausing to stare
As he did once at the mind's country.

No

And one said, This man can sing;
Let's listen to him. But the other,
Dirt on his mind, said, No, let's
Queer him. And the first, being weak,
Consented. So the Thing came
Nearer him, and its breath caused
Him to retch, and none knew why.
But he rested for one long month,
And after began to sing
For gladness, and the Thing stood,
Letting him, for a year, for two;
Then put out its raw hand
And touched him, and the wound took
Over, and the nurses wiped off
The poetry from his cracked lips.

The Observer

Catrin lives in a nice place
Of bracken, a looking-glass
For the sea that not far off
Glitters. 'You live in a nice place,
Catrin.' The eyes regard me
Unmoved; the wind fidgets
With her hair. Her tongue is a wren
Fluttering in the mouth's cage.

Here is one whom life made,
Omitting an ingredient,
For fun; for luck? How should I know
Its motives, who was not born
To question them, only to see
What I see: the golden landscape
Of nature, with the twisted creatures
Crossing it, each with his load.

Concession

Not that he brought flowers
Except for the eyes' blue,
Perishable ones, or that his hands,
Famed for kindness were put then
To such usage; but rather that, going
Through flowers later, she yet could feel
These he spared perhaps for my sake.

Sir Gelli Meurig

(Elizabethan)

I imagine it, a land
Rain-soaked, far away
In the west, in time;
The sea folded too rough
On the shingle, with hard
Breakers and steep
To climb; but game-ridden
And lining his small table
Too thickly – Gelli Meurig,
Squire of a few
Acres, but swollen-headed
With dreaming of a return
To incense, to the confections
Of worship; a Welsh fly
Caught in a web spun
For a hornet.
                        Don't blame him.
Others have turned their backs,
As he did, and do so still,
On our land. Leaves light
The autumn, but not for them.
Emptily the sea's cradle
Rocks. They want the town
And its baubles; the fine clothes
They dress one in, who manage
The strings. Helplessly they dance
To a mad tune, who at home
In the bracken could have remained
Humble but free.

Christmas

There is a morning;
Time brings it nearer,
Brittle with frost
And starlight. The owls sing
In the parishes. The people rise
And walk to the churches'
Stone lanterns, there to kneel
And eat the new bread
Of love, washing it down
With the sharp taste
Of blood they will shed.

The Green Isle

It is the sort of country that,
After leaving, one is ashamed of
Being rude about. That gentleness
Of green nature, reflected
In its people – what has one done
To deserve it? They sit about
Over slow glasses, discussing,
Not the weather, the news,
Their families, but the half
Legendary heroes of old days:
Women who gave their name
To a hill, who wore the stars
For bracelet; clanking warriors,
Shearing the waves with their swords.

That man shuffling dustily,
His pants through, to the door
Of the gin shop, is not as mean
As he looks; he has the tongue
For which ale is but the excuse
To trespass in golden meadows
Of talk, poaching his words
From the rich, but feasting on them
In that stale parlour with the zest
And freedom of a great poet.

The Fisherman

A simple man,
He liked the crease on the water
His cast made, but had no pity
For the broken backbone
Of water or fish.

One of his pleasures, thirsty,
Was to ask a drink
At the hot farms;
Leaving with a casual thank you,
As though they owed it him.

I could have told of the living water
That springs pure.
He would have smiled then,
Dancing his speckled fly in the shallows,
Not understanding.

Traeth Maelgwn

Blue sea; clouds coming up
For convention only; the marks
On the sand, that mean nothing
And don't have to to the fat,
Monoglot stranger. Maelgwn
Was here once, juggling
With the sea; there were rulers
In Wales then, men jealous
Of her honour. He put down
Rivals, made himself king
Of the waves, too; his throne
Buoyant – that rocking beacon
Its image. He kept his power
By intelligence; we lose
Ours for lack of it,
Holding our caps out
Beside a framed view
We never painted, counting
The few casual cowries
With which we are fobbed off.

Llanrhaeadr ym Mochnant

This is where he sought God.
And found him? The centuries
Have been content to follow
Down passages of serene prose.

There is no portrait of him
But in the gallery of
The imagination: a brow
With the hair's feathers
Spilled on it? a cheek
Too hollow? rows of teeth
Broken on the unmanageable bone

Of language? In this small room
By the river expiating the sin
Of his namesake?
                        The smooth words
Over which his mind flowed
Have become an heirloom. Beauty
Is how you say it, and the truth,
Like this mountain-born torrent,
Is content to hurry
Not too furiously by.

Sailors' Hospital

It was warm
Inside, but there was
Pain there. I came out
Into the cold wind
Of April. There were birds
In the brambles' old,
Jagged iron, with one striking
Its small song. To the west,
Rising from the grey
Water, leaning one
On another were the town's
Houses. Who first began
That refuse: time's waste
Growing at the edge
Of the clean sea? Some sailor,
Fetching up on the
Shingle before wind
Or current, made it his
Harbour, hung up his clothes
In the sunlight; found women
To breed from – those sick men
His descendants. Every day
Regularly the tide
Visits them with its salt
Comfort; their wounds are shrill
In the rigging of the
Tall ships.
                  With clenched thoughts,
That not even the sky's
Daffodil could persuade
To open, I turned back
To the nurses in their tugging
At him, as he drifted
Away on the current
Of his breath, further and further,
Out of hail of our love.

Reservoirs

There are places in Wales I don't go:
Reservoirs that are the subconscious
Of a people, troubled far down
With gravestones, chapels, villages even;
The serenity of their expression
Revolts me, it is a pose
For strangers, a watercolour's appeal
To the mass, instead of the poem's
Harsher conditions. There are the hills,
Too; gardens gone under the scum
Of the forests; and the smashed faces
Of the farms with the stone trickle
Of their tears down the hills' side.

Where can I go, then, from the smell
Of decay, from the putrefying of a dead
Nation? I have walked the shore
For an hour and seen the English
Scavenging among the remains
Of our culture, covering the sand
Like the tide and, with the roughness
Of the tide, elbowing our language
Into the grave that we have dug for it.

Touching

She kept touching me,
As a woman will
Accidentally, so the response,
When given, is
A presumption.
               I retained my
Balance, letting her sway
To her cost. The lips' prose
Ticked on, regulating
Her voltage.
               Such insulation!
But necessary; their flair
For some small fun with
The current being
An injustice.
It is the man burns.

The Priest

The priest picks his way
Through the parish. Eyes watch him
From windows, from the farms;
Hearts wanting him to come near.
The flesh rejects him.

Women, pouring from the black kettle,
Stir up the whirling tea-grounds
Of their thoughts; offer him a dark
Filling in their smiling sandwich.

Priests have a long way to go.
The people wait for them to come
To them over the broken glass
Of their vows, making them pay
With their sweat's coinage for their correction.

He goes up a green lane
Through growing birches; lambs cushion
His vision. He comes slowly down
In the dark, feeling the cross warp
In his hands; hanging on it his thought's icicles.

'Crippled soul,' do you say? looking at him
From the mind's height; 'limping through life
On his prayers. There are other people
In the world, sitting at table
Contented, though the broken body
And the shed blood are not on the menu.'

'Let it be so,' I say. 'Amen and amen.'

Welcome to Wales

Come to Wales
To be buried; the undertaker
Will arrange it for you. We have
The sites and a long line
Of clients going back
To the first milkman who watered
His honour. How they endow
Our country with their polished
Memorials! No one lives
In our villages, but they dream
Of returning from the rigours
Of the pound's climate. Why not
Try it? We can always raise
Some mourners, and the amens
Are ready. This is what
Chapels are for; their varnish
Wears well and will go
With most coffins. Let us
Quote you; our terms
Are the lowest, and we offer,
Dirt cheap, a place where
It is lovely to lie.

Loyalties

The prince walks upon the carpet
Our hearts have unrolled
For him; a worn carpet,
I fear. We are a poor
People; we should have saved up
For this; these rents, these blood stains,
This erosion of the edges
Of it, do him no honour.

And where does it lead to
Anyway? About the table
The shopkeepers are all attention.
I would have run it to the door
Of the holding where Puw lived
Once, wrapping the language
About him, watching the trickle
Of his children down the hill's side.

Kneeling

Moments of great calm,
Kneeling before an altar
Of wood in a stone church
In summer, waiting for the God
To speak; the air a staircase
For silence; the sun's light
Ringing me, as though I acted
A great rôle. And the audiences
Still; all that close throng
Of spirits waiting, as I,
For the message.
              Prompt me, God;
But not yet. When I speak,
Though it be you who speak
Through me, something is lost.
The meaning is in the waiting.

Tenancies

This is pain's landscape.
A savage agriculture is practised
Here; every farm has its
Grandfather or grandmother, gnarled hands
On the cheque-book, a long, slow
Pull on the placenta about the neck.
Old lips monopolise the talk
When a friend calls. The children listen
From the kitchen; the children march
With angry patience against the dawn.
They are waiting for someone to die
Whose name is as bitter as the soil
They handle. In clear pools
In the furrows they watch themselves grow old
To the terrible accompaniment of the song
Of the blackbird, that promises them love.

Art History

They made the grey stone
Blossom, setting it on a branch
Of the mind ; airy cathedrals
Grew, trembling at the tip
Of their breathing ; delicate palaces
Hung motionless in the gold,
Unbelievable sunrise. They praised
With rapt forms such as the blind hand
Dreamed, journeying to its sad
Nuptials. We come too late
On the scene, pelted with the stone
Flowers' bitter confetti.

The Small Window

In Wales there are jewels
To gather, but with the eye
Only. A hill lights up
Suddenly; a field trembles
With colour and goes out
In its turn; in one day
You can witness the extent
Of the spectrum and grow rich

With looking. Have a care;
This wealth is for the few
And chosen. Those who crowd
A small window dirty it
With their breathing, though sublime
And inexhaustible the view.

They

I take their hands,
Hard hands. There is no love
For such, only a willed
Gentleness. Negligible men
From the village, from the small
Holdings, they bring their grief
Sullenly to my back door,
And are speechless. Seeing them
In the wind with the light's
Halo, watching their eyes
Blur, I know the reason
They cry, their worsting
By one whom they will fight.

Daily the sky mirrors
The water, the water the
Sky. Daily I take their side
In their quarrel, calling their faults
Mine. How do I serve so
This being they have shut out
Of their houses, their thoughts, their lives?

Burgos

Nightingales crackled in the frost
At Burgos. The day dawned fiercely
On the parched land, on the fields to the east
Of the city, bitter with sage
And thistle. Lonely bells called
From the villages; no one answered
Them but the sad priests, fingering
Their beads, praying for the lost people
Of the soil. Everywhere were the slow
Donkeys, carrying silent men
To the mesa to reap their bundles
Of dried grass. In the air an eagle
Circled, shadowless as the God
Who made that country and drinks its blood.

Study

The flies walk upon the roof top.
The student's eyes are too keen
To miss them. The young girls walk
In the roadway; the wind ruffles
Their skirts. The student does not look.
He sees only the flies spread their wings
And take off into the sunlight
Without sound. There is nothing to do
Now but read in his book
Of how young girls walked in the roadway
In Tyre, and how young men
Sailed off into the red west
For gold, writing dry words
To the music the girls sang.

That

It will always win.
Other men will come as I have
To stand here and beat upon it
As on a door, and ask for love,
For compassion, for hatred even; for anything
Rather than this blank indifference,
Than the neutrality of its answers, if they can be called, answers
These grey skies, these wet fields,
With the wind's winding-sheet upon them.

And endlessly the days go on
With their business. Lovers make their appearance
And vanish. The germ finds its way
From the grass to the snail to the liver to the grass.
The shadow of the tree falls
On our acres like a crucifixion,
With a bird singing in the branches
What its shrill species has always sung,
Hammering its notes home
One by one into our brief flesh.

The Place

Summer is here.
Once more the house has its
Spray of martins, Proust's fountain
Of small birds, whose light shadows
Come and go in the sunshine
Of the lawn as thoughts do
In the mind. Watching them fly
Is my business, not as a man vowed
To science, who counts their returns
To the rafters, or sifts their droppings
For facts, recording the wave-length
Of their screaming; my method is so
To have them about myself
Through the hours of this brief
Season and to fill with their
Movement, that it is I they build
In and bring up their young
To return to after the bitter
Migrations, knowing the site
Inviolate through its outward changes.

Once

God looked at space and I appeared,
Rubbing my eyes at what I saw.
The earth smoked, no birds sang;
There were no footprints on the beaches
Of the hot sea, no creatures in it.
God spoke. I hid myself in the side
Of the mountain.

     As though born again
I stepped out into the cool dew,
Trying to remember the fire sermon,
Astonished at the mingled chorus
Of weeds and flowers. In the brown bark
Of the trees I saw the many faces
Of life, forms hungry for birth,
Mouthing at me. I held my way
To the light, inspecting my shadow
Boldly; and in the late morning
You, rising towards me out of the depths
Of myself. I took your hand,
Remembering you, and together,
Confederates of the natural day,
We went forth to meet the Machine.

Petition

And I standing in the shade
Have seen it a thousand times
Happen: first theft, then murder;
Rape; the rueful acts
Of the blind hand. I have said
New prayers, or said the old
In a new way. Seeking the poem
In the pain, I have learned
Silence is best, paying for it
With my conscience. I am eyes
Merely, witnessing virtue's
Defeat; seeing the young born
Fair, knowing the cancer
Awaits them. One thing I have asked
Of the disposer of the issues
Of life: that truth should defer
To beauty. It was not granted.

This One

Oh, I know it: the long story,
The ecstasies, the mutilations;
Crazed, pitiable creatures
Imagining themselves a Napoleon,
A Jesus; letting their hair grow,
Shaving it off; gorging themselves
On a dream; kindling
A new truth, withering by it.

While patiently this poor farmer
Purged himself in his strong sweat,
Ploughing under the tall boughs
Of the tree of the knowledge of
Good and evil, watching its fruit
Ripen, abstaining from it.

Echoes

What is this? said God. The obstinacy
Of its refusal to answer
Enraged him. He struck it
Those great blows it resounds
With still. It glowered at
Him, but remained dumb,
Turning on its slow axis
Of pain, reflecting the year
In its seasons. Nature bandaged
Its wounds. Healing in
The smooth sun, it became
Fair. God looked at it
Again, reminded of
An intention. They shall answer
For you, he said. And at once
There were trees with birds
Singing, and through the trees
Animals wandered, drinking
Their own scent, conceding
An absence. Where are you?
He called, and riding the echo
The shapes came, slender
As trees, but with white hands,
Curious to build. On the altars
They made him the red blood
Told what he wished to hear.

Invitation

And one voice says: Come
Back to the rain and manure
Of Siloh, to the small talk,
Of the wind, and the chapel's

Temptation; to the pale,
Sickly half-smile of
The daughter of the village
Grocer. The other says: Come

To the streets, where the pound
Sings and the doors open
To its music, with life
Like an express train running

To time. And I stay
Here, listening to them, blowing
On the small soul in my
Keeping with such breath as I have.

Period

It was a time when wise men
Were not silent, but stifled
By vast noise. They took refuge
In books that were not read.

Two counsellors had the ear
Of the public. One cried 'Buy'
Day and night, and the other,
More plausibly, 'Sell your repose.'

No Answer

But the chemicals in
My mind were not
Ready, so I let
Him go on, dissolving
The word on my
Tongue. Friend, I had said,
Life is too short for
Religion; it takes time
To prepare a sacrifice
For the God. Give yourself
To science that reveals
All, asking no pay
For it. Knowledge is power;
The old oracle
Has not changed. The nucleus
In the atom awaits
Our bidding. Come forth,
We cry, and the dust spreads
Its carpet. Over the creeds
And masterpieces our wheels go.

Song

I choose white, but with
Red on it, like the snow
In winter with its few
Holly berries and the one

Robin, that is a fire
To warm by and like Christ
Comes to us in his weakness,
But with a sharp song.

The Epitaph

You ask me what it was like?
I lived, thought, felt the temptation
Of spirit to take matter
As my invention, but bruised my mind
On the facts: the old stubbornness
Of rock, the rough bark of a tree,
The body of her I would make my own
And could not.
            And yet they ceased;
With the closing of my eyes they became
As nothing. Each day I had to begin
Their assembly, as though it were I
Who contrived them. The air was contentment
Of spirit, a glass to renew
One's illusions. Christen me, christen me,
The stone cried. Instead I bequeathed
It these words, foreseeing the forming
Of the rainbow of your brushed eyes
After the storm in my flesh.

Digest

Mostly it was wars
With their justification
Of the surrender of values
For which they fought. Between
Them they laid their plans
For the next, exempted
From compact by the machine's
Exigencies. Silence
Was out of date; wisdom consisted
In a revision of the strict code
Of the spirit. To keep moving
Was best; to bring the arrival
Nearer departure; to synchronise
The applause, as the public images
Stepped on and off the stationary
Aircraft. The labour of the years
Was over; the children were heirs
To an instant existence. They fed the machine
Their questions, knowing the answers
Already, unable to apply them.

Acting

Being unwise enough to have married her
I never knew when she was not acting.
'I love you' she would say; I heard the audiences
Sigh. 'I hate you'; I could never be sure
They were still there. She was lovely. I
Was only the looking-glass she made up in.
I husbanded the rippling meadow
Of her body. Their eyes grazed nightly upon it.

Alone now on the brittle platform
Of herself she is playing her last rôle.
It is perfect. Never in all her career
Was she so good. And yet the curtain
Has fallen. My charmer, come out from behind
It to take the applause. Look, I am clapping too.

Pavane

Convergences
Of the spirit! What
Century, love? I,
Too; you remember –
Brescia? This sunlight reminds
Of the brocade. I dined
Long. And now the music
Of darkness in your eyes
Sounds. But Brescia,
And the spreading foliage
Of smoke! With Yeats' birds
Grown hoarse.
                    Artificer
Of the years, is this
Your answer? The long dream
Unwound; we followed
Through time to the tryst
With ourselves. But wheels roll
Between and the shadow
Of the plane falls. The
Victim remains
Nameless on the tall
Steps. Master, I
Do not wish, I do not wish
To continue.

Via Negativa

Why no! I never thought other than
That God is that great absence
In our lives, the empty silence
Within, the place where we go
Seeking, not in hope to
Arrive or find. He keeps the interstices
In our knowledge, the darkness
Between stars. His are the echoes
We follow, the footprints he has just
Left. We put our hands in
His side hoping to find
It warm. We look at people
And places as though he had looked
At them, too; but miss the reflection.

Making

And having built it
I set about furnishing it
To my taste: first moss, then grass
Annually renewed, and animals
To divert me: faces stared in
From the wild. I thought up the flowers
Then birds. I found the bacteria
Sheltering in primordial
Darkness and called them forth
To the light. Quickly the earth
Teemed. Yet still an absence
Disturbed me. I slept and dreamed
Of a likeness, fashioning it,
When I woke, to a slow
Music; in love with it
For itself, giving it freedom
To love me; risking the disappointment.

The Hearth

In front of the fire
With you, the folk song
Of the wind in the chimney and the sparks'
Embroidery of the soot – eternity
Is here in this small room,
In intervals that our love
Widens; and outside
Us is time and the victims
Of time, travellers
To a new Bethlehem, statesmen
And scientists with their hands full
Of the gifts that destroy.

The Island

And God said, I will build a church here
And cause this people to worship me,
And afflict them with poverty and sickness
In return for centuries of hard work
And patience. And its walls shall be hard as
Their hearts, and its windows let in the light
Grudgingly, as their minds do, and the priest's words be drowned
By the wind's caterwauling. All this I will do,

Said God, and watch the bitterness in their eyes
Grow, and their lips suppurate with
Their prayers. And their women shall bring forth
On my altars, and I will choose the best
Of them to be thrown back into the sea.

And that was only on one island.

He

And the dogfish, spotted like God's face,
Looks at him, and the seal's eye-
Ball is cold. Autumn arrives
With birds rattling in brown showers
From hard skies. He holds out his two
Hands, calloused with the long failure
Of prayer : Take my life, he says
To the bleak sea, but the sea rejects him
Like wrack. He dungs the earth with
His children and the earth yields him
Its stone. Nothing he does, nothing he
Says is accepted, and the thin dribble
Of his poetry dries on the rocks
Of a harsh landscape under an ailing sun.

Postscript

As life improved, their poems
Grew sadder and sadder. Was there oil
For the machine? It was
The vinegar in the poets' cup.

The tins marched to the music
Of the conveyor belt. A billion
Mouths opened. Production,
Production, the wheels

Whistled. Among the forests
Of metal the one human
Sound was the lament of
The poets for deciduous language.

The River

And the cobbled water
Of the stream with the trout's indelible
Shadows that winter
Has not erased – I walk it
Again under a clean
Sky with the fish, speckled like thrushes,
Silently singing among the weed's
Branches.
         I bring the heart
Not the mind to the interpretation
Of their music, letting the stream
Comb me, feeling it fresh
In my veins, revisiting the sources
That are as near now
As on the morning I set out from them.

Female

It was the other way round:
God waved his slow wand
And the creature became a woman,
Imperceptibly, retaining its body,
Nose, brow, lips, eyes,
And the face that was like a flower
On the neck's stem. The man turned to her,
Crazy with the crushed smell
Of her hair; and her eyes warned him
To keep off. And she spoke to him with the voice
Of his own conscience, and rippled there
In the shade. So he put his hands
To his face, while her forked laughter
Played on him, and his leaves fell
Silently round him, and he hung there
On himself, waiting for the God to see.

Earth

What made us think
It was yours? Because it was signed
With your blood, God of battles?
It is such a small thing,
Easily overlooked in the multitude
Of the worlds. We are misled
By perspective; the microscope
Is our sin, we tower enormous
Above it the stronger it
Grows. Where have your incarnations
Gone to? The flesh is too heavy
To wear you, God of light
And fire. The machine replaces
The hand that fastened you
To the cross, but cannot absolve us.

All Right

I look. You look
Away. No colour,
No ruffling of the brow's
Surface betrays
Your feeling. As though I
Were not here; as
Though you were your own
Mirror, you arrange yourself
For the play. My eyes'
Adjectives; the way that
I scan you; the
Conjunction the flesh
Needs – all these
Are as nothing
To you. Serene, cool,
Motionless, no statue
Could show less
The impression of
My regard. Madam, I
Grant the artistry
Of your part. Let us
Consider it, then,
A finished performance.

Soliloquy

And God thought: Pray away,
Creatures; I'm going to destroy
It. The mistake's mine,
If you like. I have blundered
Before; the glaciers erased
My error.
       I saw them go
Further than you – palaces,
Missiles. My privacy
Was invaded; then the flaw
Took over; they allied themselves
With the dust. Winds blew away
Their pasture. Their bones signalled
From the desert to me
In vain.
       After the dust, fire;
The earth burned. I have forgotten
How long, but the fierce writing
Seduced me. I blew with my cool
Breath; the vapour condensed
In the hollows. The sun was torn
From my side. Out of the waters
You came, as subtle
As water, with your mineral
Poetry and promises
Of obedience. I listened to you
Too long. Within the churches
You built me you genuflected
To the machine. Where will it
Take you from the invisible
Viruses, the personnel
Of the darkness that do my will?

Nocturne by Ben Shahn

'Why look at me like that?'

'Well – it's your hand on the guitar.'

'Don't touch it; there is fire in it.'

'But why doesn't it burn you?'

'It does, it does; but inside me.'

'I see no smoke at your nostrils.'

'But I see green leaves at your lips.'

'They are the thoughts I would conceal.'

'You are the music that I compose.'

'Play me, then, back to myself.'

'It is too late; your face forbids it.'

'The arteries of the tall trees –'

'Are electric, charged with your blood.'

'But my hand now sleeps in my lap.'

'Let it remain so, clawed like my own.'

H'm

and one said
speak to us of love
and the preacher opened
his mouth and the word God
fell out so they tried
again speak to us
of God then but the preacher
was silent reaching
his arms out but the little
children the ones with
big bellies and bow
legs that were like
a razor shell
were too weak to come

The Kingdom

It's a long way off but inside it
There are quite different things going on:
Festivals at which the poor man
Is king and the consumptive is
Healed; mirrors in which the blind look
At themselves and love looks at them
Back; and industry is for mending
The bent bones and the minds fractured
By life. It's a long way off, but to get
There takes no time and admission
Is free, if you will purge yourself
Of desire, and present yourself with
Your need only and the simple offering
Of your faith, green as a leaf.

The Coming

And God held in his hand
A small globe. Look, he said.
The son looked. Far off,
As through water, he saw
A scorched land of fierce
Colour. The light burned
There; crusted buildings
Cast their shadows; a bright
Serpent, a river
Uncoiled itself, radiant
With slime.
         On a bare
Hill a bare tree saddened
The sky. Many people
Held out their thin arms
To it, as though waiting
For a vanished April
To return to its crossed
Boughs. The son watched
Them. Let me go there, he said.

Other

It was perfect. He could do
Nothing about it. Its waters
Were as clear as his own eye. The grass
Was his breath. The mystery
Of the dark earth was what went on
In himself. He loved and
Hated it with a parent's
Conceit, admiring his own
Work, resenting its
Independence. There were trysts
In the greenwood at which
He was not welcome. Youths and girls,
Fondling the pages of
A strange book, awakened
His envy. The mind achieved
What the heart could not. He began planning
The destruction of the long peace
Of the place. The machine appeared
In the distance, singing to itself
Of money. Its song was the web
They were caught in, men and women
Together. The villages were as flies
To be sucked empty.
         God secreted
A tear. Enough, enough,
He commanded, but the machine
Looked at him and went on singing.

The Fair

The idiot goes round and around
With his brother in a bumping-car
At the fair. The famous idiot
Smile hangs over the car's edge,
Illuminating nothing. This is mankind
Being taken for a ride by a rich
Relation. The responses are fixed:
Bump, smile; bump, smile. And the current

Is generated by the smooth flow
Of the shillings. This is an orchestra
Of steel with the constant percussion
Of laughter. But where he should be laughing
Too, his features are split open, and look!
Out of the cracks come warm, human tears.

Young and Old

Cold sea, cold sky:
This is how age looks
At a thing. The people natter,
The wind blows. Nothing they do
Is of worth. The great problems
Remain, stubborn, unsolved.
Man leaves his footprints
Momentarily on a vast shore.

And the tide comes,
That the children play with.
Ours are the first questions
They shelve. The wind is the blood
In their veins. Above them the aircraft
Domesticate the huge sky.

Boatman

A brute and
Unconscionable. He would beat,
If he had them, all
Wives, wallowing in their slopped
Kisses. Whips are too good
For such. But when I see
The waves bucking and how he sits
Them so, I think this man
A god, deserving the flowers
The sea women crown him with.

Harbour

a harbour with the
boats going in and out
at top speed their sirens
blowing and their funnels trailing
long smoke and the tousled
bluejackets of the waves emptying
their pockets to the wind's
hornpipe and far down
in the murky basements the turning
of bright bodies smooth
as a bell mermaids you
say but I say
fish

Madam

And if you ask her
She has no name;
But her eyes say,
Water is cold.

She is three years old
And willing to kiss;
But her lips say,
Apples are sour.

Omens

The queen sat on the throne of England,
   Fingering delicately the bright stones
Of its handrail. The heads rolled
   In the English dust. The queen smiled.

Meanwhile in America a Red Indian
   Fitted a coloured arrow to his bow
And took aim. The brush turkey fell
   In a storm of feathers. The Indian went home

Silently to his skin tent
   By the lake to expiate the sin
Of its killing. Over the steaming entrails
   He saw the first white man come with his guns and jails.

Relations

An ordinary lot:
The sons dwindling from a rich
Father to a house in a terrace
And furniture of the cheap sort;
The daughters respectable, marrying
Approved husbands with clean shoes
And collars; as though dullness
And nonentity's quietness
Were virtues after the crazed ways
Of that huge man, their father, buying himself
Smiles, sailing his paper money
From windows of the Welsh hotel
He had purchased to drown in drink.

But one of them was drowned
Honourably. A tale has come down
From rescuers, forced to lie off
By the breakers, of men lined up
At the rail as the ship foundered,
Smoking their pipes and bantering. And he
Was of their company; his tobacco
Stings my eyes, who am ordinary too.

Astronauts

They brought no edifying
Information back. It was the moon
Goddess they went to inspect,
Her gold hair, her gold thighs.
An absence of beauty
Oppressed them:
The flesh that was like
Pumice, a woman weary
Of hauling at
The slow tides.
                 Godhead, it
Seems, is best left
To itself; it is a fire
Extinguished, a luminary whose
Spent light reaches us still.

Islandmen

And they come sailing
From the island through the flocks
Of the sea with the boat full
Of their own flocks, brimming fleeces
And whelk eyes, with the bleating
Sea-birds and the tide races
Snarling. And the dark hull bites
At the water, crunching it
To small glass, as the men chew
Their tobacco, cleaning their mind
On wind, trusting the horizon's
Logic.
   These are the crusted men
Of the sea, measuring time
By tide-fall, knowing the changeless
Seasons, the lasting honeysuckle
Of the sea. They are lean and hard
And alert, and while our subjects
Increase, bürdening us
With their detail, these keep to the one
Fact of the sea, its pitilessness, its beauty.

Circles

A man threw some brushings away.
A wren found them and built in them.
A rat found the young when they were hatched.
The rat came, stealing the man's bread,
And lies now, a cupboard for maggots.

It is man makes the first move and the last.
He throws things away and they return to him.
He seeks things that always withdraw
And finds them waiting on his return.
He takes his departure from God
And is as trash thrown away.
But a dream finds him and builds in him,
And death comes and eats up the dreamer's
Brood. And still it is out of a man
Death is born; so before death
Man is, and after death
There is more man, and the dream outlasts
Death, and the dreamer will never die.

Experiments

I was not unhappy
At school, made something
Of the lessons over the gold heads
Of the girls. Love, said
The letters on
The blackboard. Love, I wrote down
In my book.
       There was one room,
However, that was full of
Jars, test-tubes
And wet sinks. Poisonous smells
Came from it, rumours,
Reports. The pupils who
Worked there had glasses and
Tall skulls. They were pale and
Looked at us as though we were part
Of a boring experiment.

The Country

About living in the country?
I yawn; that step, for instance –
No need to look up – Evans
On his way to the fields, where he hoes
Up one row of mangolds and down
The next one. You needn't wonder
What goes on in his mind, there is nothing
Going on there; the unemployment
Of the lobes is established. His small dole
Is kindness of the passers-by
Who mister him, who read an answer
To problems in the way his speech
Comes haltingly, and his eyes reflect
Stillness. I would say to them
About living in the country, peace
Can deafen one, beauty surprise
No longer. There is only the thud
Of the slow foot up the long lane
At morning and back at night.

Castaway

I have no name for today
But itself. Long ago
I lost count of the days.
Castaways have no mirror
But the sea, that leaves its wrinkles
On themselves, too. Every morning
I see how the sun comes up
Unpublicised; there are no news
On this beach. What I do
Neither the tall birds on the shore,
Nor the animals in the bush
Care about. They have all time
And no time, each one about
Its business, foraging, breeding.
I thought that they had respect
For a human. Here there are creatures
That jostle me, others that crawl
On my loved flesh. I am the food
They were born for, endlessly shrilling
Their praises. I have seen the bones
In the jungle, that are the cradle
We came from and go back to.

Seaside

And the sea opens its bag
On the sand. I didn't ask
To be born, screams the child,
Paddling. The grown girl

Smiles, helping herself
To its trinkets. The men leer.
On the horizon the shark's
Fin passes, a dark sail.

The Sea

They wash their hands in it.
The salt turns to soap
In their hands. Wearing it
At their wrists, they make bracelets
Of it; it runs in beads
On their jackets. A child's
Plaything? It has hard whips
That it cracks, and knuckles
To pummel you. It scrubs
And scours; it chews rocks
To sand; its embraces
Leave you without breath. Mostly
It is a stomach, where bones,
Wrecks, continents are digested.

I

I imagine it: Two people,
A bed; I was not
There. They dreamed of me?
No, they sought themselves
In the other, You,
They breathed. I overheard
From afar. I was nine months
Coming ... nearer, nearer;
The ugliness of the place
Daunted. I hung back
In the dark, but was cast out,
Howling. Love, they promised;
It will be love and sunlight
And joy. I took their truth
In my mouth and mumbled it
For a while, till my teeth
Grew. Ah, they cried, so you would,
Would you? I knew the cold
Of the world and preferred warmth
To freedom. I let the cord
Hang, the lawn my
Horizon. Girls came
And stared at me, but her eyes
Cowed me. Duty,
They shrilled. I saw how their lives
Frayed, and praised myself
For emotion, swallowing
My snivel.
       Years went by;
I escaped, but never outgrew
The initial contagion.

The Smile

My mother prayed that I should have the sweet tooth.
My father said that I should have the big fist.
And life, lingering somewhere by,
Smiled on me, giving me neither.

Asides

And at Carcassonne I was looking
At the cats on the river
Tow-path. How they ran,
Male and female, faster

Than the smooth river through
Hoops of light; so I forgot
The castle and the long wars
Of kings and princes and

The philosopher's question, even
My own need for
Conviction. And the mice sang
In the dew, as though they agreed with me.

Lost Christmas

He is alone, it is Christmas.
Up the hill go three trees, the three kings.
There is a star also
Over the dark manger. But where is the Child?

Pity him. He has come far
Like the trees, matching their patience
With his. But the mind was before
Him on the long road. The manger is empty.

If You Can Call it Living

In Wales there are
no crocodiles, but the tears
continue to flow from
their slimed sources. Women
with white hair and strawberry
faces peer at you from behind
curtains; wobbling sopranos
split the chapels; the clerks undress
the secretaries with
their lean eyes.
                    Who will employ
the loafers at the street
corners, choking over
the joke's phlegm?
                    Anything to
sell? cries the tourist
to the native rummaging among
the remnants of his self-respect.

Somewhere to Go for a Laugh

I am not from these parts.
My auntie's is the next house
but one in the next village
but one in the next
county. If you hear me use
English, it is not for you to judge
the accent. I have ways, too,
of getting about; my nose tells
the seasons, as your calendars do.
I am more equal; in twelve towns
under the grinding of the shillings
I have heard the muse purr. My father
was after all one of those born
to preferment – Rural Dean
of the Bottom Hundred I have known him called.

To Pay for His Keep

So this was on the way
to a throne! He looked round
at the perspiring ranks
of ageing respectables:
police, tradesmen, councillors,
rigid with imagined
loyalty; and beyond them at
the town with its mean streets and
pavements filthy with
dog shit.
      The castle was
huge. All that dead weight
of the past, that overloading
of the law's mounting
equipment! A few medals
would do now. He permitted
himself a small smile,
sipping at it in the mind's
coolness.
      And never noticed,
because of the dust raised
by the prayers of the fagged
clergy, that far hill
in the sun with the long line
of its trees climbing
it like a procession
of young people, young as himself.

He Lies Down to be Counted

And in Tregaron Henry Richard
still freezes, cast in shame to preside
over the pacifism of a servile people.

Thomas Charles, too, has seen the Bible
petrified. Nothing can stir the pages
of the book he holds; not even the draught from Tryweryn.

In our country you make your way
from monument to monument. Besides
the villages' and the towns'

statues, there are the memories of those others
who gave their lives for the freedom
to make money, the innumerable Joneses

and Owens, who might have brought our blood
to the boil; who are clothed now
in the indiscriminate mufti of the soil.

His Condescensions Are Short-Lived

I don't know, he said. I feel sorry
for the English – a fine people
in some ways, but victims
of their traditions. All those tanks
and guns; the processions
that go nowhere; the medals
and gold braid; the government's
yearly awards; the replenishment
of the clapped ranks of
the peerage. Democracy is the tip
the rich and the well-born give
for your homage.
               I admired him
there, as he sat nonchalantly
in his chair, flicking the ash from
his cigarette – supplied, by the way,
as most things in Wales are
supplied, by English wholesalers.

The Earth Does its Best for Him

The paintings are under glass,
or in dry rooms it is difficult
to breathe in; they are tired
of returning the hard stare
of eyes. The sculptures are smooth
from familiarity. There is a smell
of dust, the precipitation
of culture from dead skies.

I return to Lleyn,
repository of the condescension
of time. Through the car's
open windows the scent of hay
comes. It is incense, the seasonally
renewed offering of the live earth.

He Agrees with Henry Ford

Llywelyn? Old hat.
Glyndwr? A con man,
Iolo licking his arse
for a doublet, for his next
meal.
      Rusty their armour,
yellow their bones, let them
brag in the safety of the dry
libraries. Honours forbid
that they should start their nonsense.

Rising sixty, my post-war
credits are due, my feet
are towards the electric
fire; my favourite programme
begins. I have drawn the curtains
on the raw sky where our history
bleeds, where Cilgwri's ousel
on my ramshackle aerial
keeps the past's goal
against the balls of tomorrow.

It Hurts Him to Think

The decree went forth
    to destroy the language – 'not cariad'
they said, 'love'. The nursing future
    saw the tightening lips
of the English drawn on the hard sky
    to the east. 'You can have the job,
if you ask for it in the right
    words.' 'Come buy, come buy,'
tolled the bells of the churches
    in the new towns. The Welsh
put on their best clothes
    and took their produce
to market, and brought it back
    with them, unsold. 'We want
nothing from you but your
    land.' The heiresses fell
for the velvet businessmen
    of the shires. The peasantry
saw their pastures fenced in
    with the bones of heroes. The
industrialists came, burrowing
    in the corpse of a nation
for its congealed blood. I was
    born into the squalor of
their feeding and sucked their speech
    in with my mother's
infected milk, so that whatever
    I throw up now is still theirs.

Emerging

Not as in the old days I pray,
God. My life is not what it was.
Yours, too, accepts the presence of
the machine? Once I would have asked
healing. I go now to be doctored,
to drink sinlessly of the blood
of my brother, to lend my flesh
as manuscript of the great poem
of the scalpel. I would have knelt
long, wrestling with you, wearing
you down. Hear my prayer, Lord, hear
my prayer. As though you were deaf, myriads
of mortals have kept up their shrill
cry, explaining your silence by
their unfitness.
                It begins to appear
this is not what prayer is about.
It is the annihilation of difference,
the consciousness of myself in you,
of you in me; the emerging
from the adolescence of nature
into the adult geometry
of the mind. I begin to recognise
you anew, God of form and number.
There are questions we are the solution
to, others whose echoes we must expand
to contain. Circular as our way
is, it leads not back to that snake-haunted
garden, but onward to the tall city
of glass that is the laboratory of the spirit.

The Hand

It was a hand. God looked at it
and looked away. There was a coldness
about his heart, as though the hand
clasped it. As at the end
of a dark tunnel, he saw cities
the hand would build, engines
that it would raze them with. His sight
dimmed. Tempted to undo the joints
of the fingers, he picked it up.
But the hand wrestled with him. 'Tell
me your name,' it cried, 'and I will write it
in bright gold. Are there not deeds
to be done, children to make, poems
to be written? The world
is without meaning, awaiting
my coming.' But God, feeling the nails
in his side, the unnerving warmth
of the contact, fought on in
silence. This was the long war with himself
always foreseen, the question not
to be answered. What is the hand
for? The immaculate conception
preceding the delivery
of the first tool? 'I let you go,'
he said, 'but without blessing.
Messenger to the mixed things
of your making, tell them I am.'

The Word

A pen appeared, and the god said:
'Write what it is to be
man.' And my hand hovered
long over the bare page,

until there, like footprints
of the lost traveller, letters
took shape on the page's
blankness, and I spelled out

the word 'lonely'. And my hand moved
to erase it; but the voices
of all those waiting at life's
window cried out loud: 'It is true.'

Out There

It is another country.
There is no speech there such
as we know; even the colours

are different.
When the residents use their eyes,
it is not shapes they see but the distance
between them. If they go,
it is not in a traveller's
usual direction, but sideways and
out through the mirror of a refracted
timescale. If you met them early,
you would recognise them by an absence
of shadow. Your problems

are in their past;
those they are about to solve
are what you are incapable
of conceiving. In experiments
in outbreeding, under the growing microscope
of the mind, they are isolating
the human virus and burning it
up in the fierceness of their detachment.

Amen

It was all arranged:
the virgin with child, the birth
in Bethlehem, the arid journey uphill
to Jerusalem. The prophets foretold
it, the scriptures conditioned him
to accept it. Judas went to his work
with his sour kiss; what else
could he do?
          A wise old age,
the honours awarded for lasting,
are not for a saviour. He had
to be killed; salvation acquired
by an increased guilt. The tree,
with its roots in the mind's dark,
was divinely planted, the original fork
in existence. There is no meaning in life,
unless men can be found to reject
love. God needs his martyrdom.
The mild eyes stare from the Cross
in perverse triumph. What does he care
that the people's offerings are so small?

God's Story

A thousand years went by.
The Buddha sat under the Bo tree
rhyming. God burned in the sky

as of old. The family waited
for him who would not come back
any more. Who is my father

and mother? God fingered the hole
in his side, where the green tree
came from. The desert gave up

its saints. The Pope's ring was deadly
as a snake's kiss. Art and poetry
drank of that slow poison. God,

looking into a dry chalice,
felt the cold touch of the machine
on his hand, leading him

to a steel altar. 'Where are you?'
he called, seeking himself among
the dumb cogs and tireless camshafts.

Relay

I switch on, tune in –
the marvellous languages
of the peoples of the planet,
discussing the weather! Thousands of years
speech was evolving – that line of trees
on the hill slope has the illusion
of movement. I think of man
on his mountain; he has paused
now for lack of the oxygen
of the spirit; the easier options
surround him, the complacencies of being
half-way up. He needs some breath
from the summit, a stench rising
to him from the valley from
which he has toiled to release
his potential; a memory rather
of those bright flags, that other
climbers of other mountains
have planted and gone
their way, not down but on
up the incline of their choosing.

The Prayer

He kneeled down
           dismissing his orisons
as inappropriate; one by one
           they came to his lips and were swallowed
but without bile.
           He fell back
on an old prayer: Teach me to know
           what to pray for. He
listened; after the weather of
           his asking, no still, small
voice, only the parade
           of ghosts, casualties
of his past intercessions. He
           held out his hands, cupped
as though to receive blood, leaking
           from life's side. They
remained dry, as his mouth
           did. But the prayer formed:
Deliver me from the long drought
           of the mind. Let leaves
from the deciduous Cross
           fall on us, washing
us clean, turning our autumn
           to gold by the affluence of their fountain.

The Tool

So there was nothing?
Nothing. An echo?
Who spoke? There was emptiness
and a face staring, seeking
a likeness. There was thought
probing an absence. God
knew he was naked and
withdrew himself. And the germs
swarmed, their alphabet
lengthened; where was the tongue
to pronounce it? Pain, said
the voice, and the creature
stood up, its mind folded
on darkness. It put out a hand,
as though to implore
wisdom, and a tool
gleamed there. The alternatives
of the tree sharpened. God
spoke to him out of the tree's
wholeness, but the sound
of the tool drowned him. He came forth
in his nakedness. 'Forgive me,'
he said, suffering the tool's
insolence in his own body.

Poste Restante

I want you to know how it was,
whether the Cross grinds into dust
under men's wheels or shines brightly
as a monument to a new era.

There was a church and one man
served it, and few worshipped
there in the raw light on the hill
in winter, moving among the stones
fallen about them like the ruins
of a culture they were too weak
to replace, too poor themselves
to do anything but wait
for the ending of a life
they had not asked for.
           The priest would come
and pull on the hoarse bell nobody
heard, and enter that place
of darkness, sour with the mould
of the years. And the spider would run
from the chalice, and the wine lie
there for a time, cold and unwanted
by all but he, while the candles
guttered as the wind picked
at the roof. And he would see
over that bare meal his face
staring at him from the cracked glass
of the window, with the lips moving
like those of an inhabitant of
a world beyond this.
           And so back
to the damp vestry to the book
where he would scratch his name and the date
he could hardly remember, Sunday
by Sunday, while the place sank
to its knees and the earth turned
from season to season like the wheel
of a great foundry to produce
you, friend, who will know what happened.

Woman Combing

Degas

So the hair, too,
             can be played?

She lets it down
             and combs a sonata

from it: brown cello
             of hair, with the arm

bowing. Painter,
             who with your quick

brush, gave us this silent
             music, there is nothing

that you left out.
             The blues and greens,

the abandoned snowfall
             of her shift, the light

on her soft flesh tell us
             from what score she performs.

The Son

It was your mother wanted you;
you were already half-formed
when I entered. But can I deny
the hunger, the loneliness bringing me in
from myself? And when you appeared
before me, there was no repentance
for what I had done, as there was shame
in the doing it; compassion only
for that which was too small to be called
human. The unfolding of your hands
was plant-like, your ear was the shell
I thundered in; your cries, when they came,
were those of a blind creature
trodden upon; pain not yet become grief.

Mediations

And to one God says: Come
to me by numbers and
figures; see my beauty
in the angles between
stars, in the equations
of my kingdom. Bring
your lenses to the worship
of my dimensions: far
out and far in, there
is always more of me
in proportion. And to another:
I am the bush burning
at the centre of
your existence; you must put
your knowledge off and come
to me with your mind
bare. And to this one
he says: Because of
your high stomach, the bleakness
of your emotions, I
will come to you in the simplest
things, in the body
of a man hung on a tall
tree you have converted to
timber and you shall not know me.

The Chapel

A little aside from the main road,
becalmed in a last-century greyness,
there is the chapel, ugly, without the appeal
to the tourist to stop his car
and visit it. The traffic goes by,
and the river goes by, and quick shadows
of clouds, too, and the chapel settles
a little deeper into the grass.

But here once on an evening like this,
in the darkness that was about
his hearers, a preacher caught fire
and burned steadily before them
with a strange light, so that they saw
the splendour of the barren mountains
about them and sang their amens
fiercely, narrow but saved
in a way that men are not now.

The Casualty

I had forgotten
        the old quest for truth
                I was here for. Other cares

held me: urgencies
        of the body; a girl
                beckoned; money

had never appeared
        so ethereal; it was God's blood
                circulating in the veins

of creation; I partook
        of it like Communion, lost
                myself on my way

home, with the varying voices
        on call. Moving backward
                into a receding

future, I lost the use
        of perspective, borrowing poetry
                to buy my children

their prose. The past was a poor
        king, rendering his crown down
                for the historian. Every day

I went on with that
        metallic warfare in which
                the one casualty is love.

The Problem

There was this problem.
The mind contemplated it;
the body amused itself
in the sun. Put it by, put it by,
the wind whispered. The mind
dozed. Seven empires went under
the blown sand. A people stood up
in Athens; the problem recognised
them, but was not to be outstared
by their blind sculpture. Son of God
or Son of Man? At Jerusalem
the problem was given a new shape.
The Cross offered its gaunt solution
to the Gentiles; under its shadow
their bones whitened. The philosophers christened
their premise. The problem reposed
over the cellars of the alchemists.

Probing

No one would know you had lived,
but for my discovery
of the anonymous undulation
of your grave, like the early swelling
of the belly of a woman
who is with child. And if I entered
it now, I would find your bones
huddled together, but without
flesh, their ruined architecture
a reproach, the skull luminous
but not with thought.
               Would it help us to learn
what you were called in your forgotten
language? Are not our jaws
frail for the sustaining of the consonants'
weight? Yet they were balanced
on tongues like ours, echoed
in the ears' passages, in intervals when
the volcano was silent. How
tenderly did the woman handle
them, as she leaned her haired body
to yours? Where are the instruments
of your music, the pipe of hazel, the
bull's horn, the interpreters
of your loneliness on this
ferocious planet?
               We are domesticating
it slowly; but at times it rises
against us, so that we see again
the primeval shadows you built
your fire amongst. We are cleverer
than you; our nightmares
are intellectual. But we never awaken
from the compulsiveness of the mind's
stare into the lenses' furious interiors.

The Flower

I asked for riches.
You gave me the earth, the sea,
                    the immensity
of the broad sky. I looked at them
and learned I must withdraw
            to possess them. I gave my eyes
            and my ears, and dwelt
in a soundless darkness
                    in the shadow
            of your regard.
                    The soul
            grew in me, filling me
with its fragrance.
                    Men came
to me from the four
            winds to hear me speak
            of the unseen flower by which
I sat, whose roots were not
in the soil, nor its petals the colour
of the wide sea; that was
            its own species with its own
            sky over it, shot
with the rainbow of your coming and going.

Ann Griffith

So God spoke to her,
she the poor girl from the village
without learning. 'Play me,'
he said, 'on the white keys
of your body. I have seen you dance
for the bridegrooms that were not
to be, while I waited for you
under the ripening boughs of
the myrtle. These people know me
only in the thin hymns of
the mind, in the arid sermons
and prayers. I am the live God,
nailed fast to the old tree
of a nation by its unreal
tears. I thirst, I thirst
for the spring water. Draw it up
for me from your heart's well and I will change
it to wine upon your unkissed lips.

The Moon in Lleyn

The last quarter of the moon
of Jesus gives way
to the dark; the serpent
digests the egg. Here
on my knees in this stone
church, that is full only
of the silent congregation
of shadows and the sea's
sound, it is easy to believe
Yeats was right. Just as though
choirs had not sung, shells
have swallowed them; the tide laps
at the Bible; the bell fetches
no people to the brittle miracle
of the bread. The sand is waiting
for the running back of the grains
in the wall into its blond
glass. Religion is over, and
what will emerge from the body
of the new moon, no one
can say.
       But a voice sounds
in my ear: Why so fast,
mortal? These very seas
are baptised. The parish
has a saint's name time cannot
unfrock. In cities that
have outgrown their promise people
are becoming pilgrims
again, if not to this place,
then to the recreation of it
in their own spirits. You must remain
kneeling. Even as this moon
making its way through the earth's
cumbersome shadow, prayer, too,
has its phases.

Suddenly

As I had always known
he would come, unannounced,
remarkable merely for the absence
of clamour. So truth must appear
to the thinker; so, at a stage
of the experiment, the answer
must quietly emerge. I looked
at him, not with the eye
only, but with the whole
of my being, overflowing with
him as a chalice would
with the sea. Yet was he
no more there than before,
his area occupied
by the unhaloed presences.
You could put your hand
in him without consciousness
of his wounds. The gamblers
at the foot of the unnoticed
cross went on with
their dicing; yet the invisible
garment for which they played
was no longer at stake, but worn
by him in this risen existence.

Taste

I had preferred Chaucer
but for the slop in his saucer;

or grave Edmund Spenser
moving formally as a dancer.

But Shakespeare's cut and thrust,
I allow you, was a must

on my bookshelves; and after,
Donne's thin, cerebral laughter.

Dryden I could not abide,
nor the mincing fratricide

of Pope. Jonathan Swift,
though courageous, had no uplift.

But Wordsworth, looking in the lake
of his mind, him I could take;

and Percy Shelley at times;
Byron, too, but only for his rhymes.

Tennyson? Browning? If I mention
them, it is but from convention,

despite the vowel technique
of the one, the other's moral cheek.

Then Hardy, for many a major
poet, is for me just an old-stager,

shuffling about a bogus heath
cobwebbed with his Victorian breath.

And coming to my own century
with its critics' compulsive hurry

to place a poet, I must smile
at the congestion at the turnstile

of fame, the faceless, formless amoeba
with the secretion of its *vers libre*.

Rough

God looked at the eagle that looked at
the wolf that watched the jack-rabbit
cropping the grass, green and curling
as God's beard. He stepped back;
it was perfect, a self-regulating machine
of blood and faeces. One thing was missing:
he skimmed off a faint reflection of himself
in sea-water; breathed air into it,
and set the red corpuscles whirling. It was not long
before the creature had the eagle, the wolf and
the jack-rabbit squealing for mercy. Only the grass
resisted. It used it to warm its imagination
by. God took a handful of small germs,
sowing them in the smooth flesh. It was curious,
the harvest: the limbs modelled an obscene
question, the head swelled, out of the eyes came
tears of pus. There was the sound
of thunder, the loud, uncontrollable laughter of
God, and in his side like an incurred stitch, Jesus.

The Gap

The one thing they were not troubled
by was perfection; it was theirs
already. Their hand moved in the dark
like a priest's, giving its blessing
to the bare wall. Drawings appeared
there like a violation of the privacy
of the creatures. They withdrew with their work
finished, leaving the interrogation of it
to ourselves, who inherit everything
but their genius.
                This was before
the fall. Somewhere between them and us
the mind climbed up into the tree
of knowledge, and saw the forbidden subjects
of art, the emptiness of the interiors
of the mirror that life holds up
to itself, and began venting its frustration
in spurious metals, in the cold acts of the machine.

The Annunciation
by Veneziano

The messenger is winged
                and the girl
haloed a distance
              between them
and between them and us
down the long path the door
through which he has not
                  come
on his lips what all women
                desire to hear
in his hand the flowers that
              he has taken from her.

Ivan Karamazov

Yes, I know what he is like:
a kind of impossible robot
you insert your prayers into
like tickets, that after a while
are returned to you with the words
'Not granted' written upon them.
I repudiate such a god.
But if, as you say, he exists,
and what I do is an offence
to him, let him punish me:
I shall not squeal; to be proved
right is worth a lifetime's
chastisement. And to have God
avenging himself is to have
the advantage, till the earth opens
to receive one into a dark
cleft, where, safer than Elijah,
one will know him trumpeting
in the wind and the fire
and the roar of the earthquake, but not
in the still, small voice of the
worms that deliver one for ever
out of the tyranny of his self-love.

Hill Christmas

They came over the snow to the bread's
purer snow, fumbled it in their huge
hands, put their lips to it
like beasts, stared into the dark chalice
where the wine shone, felt it sharp
on their tongue, shivered as at a sin
remembered, and heard love cry
momentarily in their hearts' manger.

They rose and went back to their poor
holdings, naked in the bleak light
of December. Their horizon contracted
to the one small, stone-riddled field
with its tree, where the weather was nailing
the appalled body that had asked to be born.

The Combat

You have no name.
We have wrestled with you all
day, and now night approaches,
the darkness from which we emerged
seeking; and anonymous
you withdraw, leaving us nursing
our bruises, our dislocations.

For the failure of language
there is no redress. The physicists
tell us your size, the chemists
the ingredients of your
thinking. But who you are
does not appear, nor why
on the innocent marches
of vocabulary you should choose
to engage us, belabouring us
with your silence. We die, we die
with the knowledge that your resistance
is endless at the frontier of the great poem.

Ffynon Fair

(St Mary's Well)

They did not divine it, but
they bequeathed it to us:
clear water, brackish at times,
complicated by the white frosts
of the sea, but thawing quickly.

Ignoring my image, I peer down
to the quiet roots of it, where
the coins lie, the tarnished offerings
of the people to the pure spirit
that lives there, that has lived there
always, giving itself up
to the thirsty, withholding
itself from the superstition
of others, who ask for more.

Somewhere

Something to bring back to show
you have been there: a lock of God's
hair, stolen from him while he was
asleep; a photograph of the garden
of the spirit. As has been said,
the point of travelling is not
to arrive, but to return home
laden with pollen you shall work up
into the honey the mind feeds on.

What are our lives but harbours
we are continually setting out
from, airports at which we touch
down and remain in too briefly
to recognise what it is they remind
us of? And always in one
another we seek the proof
of experiences it would be worth dying for.

Surely there is a shirt of fire
this one wore, that is hung up now
like some rare fleece in the hall of heroes?
Surely these husbands and wives
have dipped their marriages in a fast
spring? Surely there exists somewhere,
as the justification for our looking for it,
the one light that can cast such shadows?

Marged

Was she planned?
Or is this one of life's
throw-offs? Small, taken from school
young; put to minister
to a widowed mother, who keeps
her simple, she feeds the hens,
speaks their language, is one
of them, quick, easily
frightened, with sharp
eyes, ears. When I have
been there, she keeps her perch
on my mind. I would
stroke her feathers, quieten
her, say: 'Life is
like this.' But have I
the right, who have seen plainer
women with love
in abundance, with
freedom, with money to
hand? If there is one thing
she has, it is a bird's
nature, volatile
as a bird. But even
as those among whom she
lives and moves, who look at her
with their expectant
glances, song is denied her.

Thus

Whatever you imagine
has happened. No words
are unspoken, no actions
undone: wine poisoned

in the chalice, the corpses
raped. While Isaiah's
angel hither and thither
flies with his hot coal.

Alive

It is alive. It is you,
God. Looking out I can see
no death. The earth moves, the
sea moves, the wind goes
on its exuberant
journeys. Many creatures
reflect you, the flowers
your colour, the tides the precision
of your calculations. There
is nothing too ample
for you to overflow, nothing
so small that your workmanship
is not revealed. I listen
and it is you speaking.
I find the place where you lay
warm. At night, if I waken,
there are the sleepless conurbations
of the stars. The darkness
is the deepening shadow
of your presence; the silence a
process in the metabolism
of the being of love.

Which

And in the book I read:
God is love. But lifting
my head, I do not find it
so. Shall I return

to my book and, between
print, wander an air
heavy with the scent
of this one word? Or not trust

language, only the blows that
life gives me, wearing them
like those red tokens with which
an agreement is sealed?

Gone

There was a flower blowing
and a hand plucked it.

There was a stream flowing
and a body smirched it.

There was a pure mirror
of water and a face came

and looked in it. There were words
and wars and treaties, and feet trampled

the earth and the wheels
seared it; and an explosion

followed. There was dust
and silence; and out of the dust

a plant grew, and the dew formed
upon it; and a stream seeped

from the dew to construct
a mirror, and the mirror was empty.

Pardon

What pardon for this, Lord?

There was a man ate bread
from your hand and did not snap
at it; but when on his knees
listened to the snivelling sound
of laughter from somewhere inside
himself. He had been taught
that to laugh was an echo
of the divine joy; but this
was the lifting of a dog's leg
in a temple. There is no defence
against laughter issuing
at the wrong time, but is there ever
forgiveness?
        He went from his prayers
into a world holding
its sides, but the return
to them was the return
to vomit, thanking where
he did not believe for something
he did not want but could not
refuse.
        There is no pardon
for this, only the expedient
of blaming the laughter on someone else.

Marriage

I look up; you pass.
I have to reconcile your
existence and the meaning of it
with what I read: kings and queens
and their battles
for power. You have your battle,
too. I ask myself: Have
I been on your side? Lovelier
a dead queen than a live
wife? History worships
the fact but cannot remain
neutral. Because there are no kings
worthy of you; because poets
better than I are not here
to describe you; because time
is always too short, you must go by
now without mention, as unknown
to the future as to
the past, with one man's
eyes resting on you
in the interval of his concern.

Montrose

It is said that he went gaily to that scaffold,
dressed magnificently as a bridegroom,
his lace lying on him like white frost
in the windless morning of his courage.

His red blood was the water of life,
changed to wine at the wedding banquet;
the bride Scotland, the spirit dependent on
such for the consummation of her marriage.

The Bright Field

I have seen the sun break through
to illuminate a small field
for a while, and gone my way
and forgotten it. But that was the pearl
of great price, the one field that had
the treasure in it. I realize now
that I must give all that I have
to possess it. Life is not hurrying

on to a receding future, nor hankering after
an imagined past. It is the turning
aside like Moses to the miracle
of the lit bush, to a brightness
that seemed as transitory as your youth
once, but is the eternity that awaits you.

Now

Men, who in their day
went down acknowledging
defeat, what would they say
now, where no superlatives
have meaning? What was failure
to them, our abandonment
of an ideal has turned
into high art. Could
they with foreknowledge have
been happy? Can we,
because there are levels
not yet descended to,
take comfort? Is it
sufficient for us
that we, like that minority
of our fellows in the hurrying
centuries, turning aside
re-enter the garden? What
is the serenity of art
worth without the angels
at the hot gates, whose sword
is time and our uneasy conscience?

Llananno

I often call there.
There are no poems in it
for me. But as a gesture
of independence of the speeding
traffic I am a part
of, I stop the car,
turn down the narrow path
to the river, and enter
the church with its clear reflection
beside it.
       There are few services
now; the screen has nothing
to hide. Face to face
with no intermediary
between me and God, and only the water's
quiet insistence on a time
older than man, I keep my eyes
open and am not dazzled,
so delicately does the light enter
my soul from the serene presence
that waits for me till I come next.

The Interrogation

But the financiers will ask
in that day: Is it not better
to leave broken bank balances
behind us than broken heads?

And Christ recognising the
new warriors will feel breaching
his healed side their terrible
pencil and the haemorrhage of its figures.

Sea-watching

Grey waters, vast
      as an area of prayer
that one enters. Daily
      over a period of years
I have let the eye rest on them.
Was I waiting for something?
                Nothing
but that continuous waving
      that is without meaning
occurred.
      Ah, but a rare bird is
rare. It is when one is not looking,
at times one is not there
            that it comes.
You must wear your eyes out,
as others their knees.
      I became the hermit
of the rocks, habited with the wind
and the mist. There were days,
so beautiful the emptiness
it might have filled,
          its absence
was as its presence; not to be told
any more, so single my mind
after its long fast,
        my watching from praying.

Good *→ that good night*

The old man comes out on the hill
and looks down to recall earlier days
in the valley. He sees the stream shine,
the church stand, hears the litter of
children's voices. A chill in the flesh
tells him that death is not far off
now: it is the shadow under the great boughs
of life. His garden has herbs growing.
The kestrel goes by with fresh prey
in its claws. The wind scatters the scent
of wild beans. The tractor operates
on the earth's body. His grandson is there
ploughing; his young wife fetches him
cakes and tea and a dark smile. It is well.

Travellers

I think of the continent
of the mind. At some stage
in the crossing of it a traveller
rejoiced. This is the truth,
he cried; I have won
my salvation!
                  What was it like
to be alive then? Was it a time
when two sparrows were sold
for a farthing? What recipe
did he bequeath us for the solution
of our problems other than the statement
of his condition? The territory
has expanded since then. We
see now that the journey is
without end, and there is no joy
in the knowledge. Going on, going
back, standing aside – the alternatives
are appalling, as is the imagining
of the lost traveller, what he would
say to us, if he were here
now, and how discredited we would find it.

Resolution

The new year brings the old resolve
to be brave, to be patient,
to suffer the betrayal of birth
without flinching, without bitter
words. The way in was hard;
the way out could be made
easy, but one must not take
it; must await decay perhaps
of the mind, certainly of the mind's
image of itself that it has
projected. The bone aches, the blood
limps like a cripple about the ruins
of one's body. Yet what are these
but the infirmities that we share
with the creatures? It is the memories
that one has, the impenitent bungler
of love, refusing for too long
to say 'yes' to that earlier gesture
of love that had brought one
forth; it is these, as they grow
clearer with the telescoping
of the years, that constitute
for the beholder the true human pain.

In Memory

I dislike the convention
but I place this stone here
in memory of those afternoons
when they slept, when happiness descended

an invisible staircase
of air, and the surf of their snoring
parted to reveal the shore
I must make for. A child

has scarcely the right
to forgive its parents. They were not bad,
wrong only, proud as
their neighbours of the necessity

of being so. Even the gaps
in their taste were windows on
to a wider world. The ornaments smile
from the past. There is no hatred

here, merely a bitter affection
for the thoroughness of their scrubbing
of a boy's body against
the contagion of the interior mind.

Two

So you have to think
of the bone hearth where love
was kindled, of the size
of the shadows so small a flame
threw on the world's
walls, with the heavens
over them, lighting their vaster fires
to no end. He took her hand
sometimes and felt the will to be
of the poetry he could not
write. She measured him
with her moist eye for the coat
always too big. And time,
the faceless collector
of taxes, beat on their thin
door, and they opened
to him, looking beyond
him, beyond the sediment
of his myriad demands to the
bright place, where their undaunted
spirits were already walking.

The Valley Dweller

He heard that there were other places
but he never saw them. No travellers
came back to him with gold on their boots,
with sand even. What was his life
worth? Was there a tree he did not eat
of, because he was not tempted
to? And must we praise him for it?

I have visited his valley:
beautiful enough, the trees' braziers
alight, the clouds tall, the river,
coming from somewhere far off, hurrying
where? Is wisdom refraining
from thinking about it? And is there
the one question we must not put?

He looked in this mirror, saw that
for all its wateriness his image
was not erased; listened while
life lasted to what it seemed
to be saying to him between
two sides of a valley, which
was not much, but sufficient for him.

Eheu! Fugaces

One year for Llew the spear
was in the making, for us
how many the viruses
that will finish us off?
                              Meanwhile
with our ear to history's
curved shell we listen
to mixed sounds. No recipe
there. The facts are neutral
and to be endured. Lorca
was innocent and died
young. Francis the emperor
of the Austrians, first
gentleman of Europe, bloodless
and out of touch, lived
on, setting his hand
to the barbed treaties.
                              Between
one story and another
what difference but in the telling
of it? And this life
that we lead, will it sound
well on the future's
cassette? I see the wise man
with his mouth open shouting
inaudibly on this side of the abyss.

The Listener in the Corner

Last night the talk
was of the relationship of the self
to God, tonight of God
to the self. The centuries
yawn. Alone in the corner
one sits whose silence persuades
of the pointlessness
of the discourse. He drinks
at another fountain that builds
itself equally from the dust of ruffians
and saints. Outside the wind
howls; the stars, that once
were the illuminated city
of the imagination, to him are fires
extinguished before the eyes' lenses
formed. The universe
is a large place with more of
darkness than light. But slowly
a web is spun there as minds like
his swing themselves to and fro.

Almost

Was here and was one person
and was not; knew hunger
and its excess and was too full
for words; was memory's
victim. Had he a hand
in himself? He had two
that were not his: with one
he would build, with the other
he would knock down. The earth
catered for him and he drank
blood. What was the mirror
he looked in? Over his shoulder
he saw fear, on the horizon
its likeness. A woman paused
for him on her way
nowhere and together they
made in the great darkness the
small fire that is life's decoy.

Incense

The disingenuousness
of the dawn, showing everything
it possesses even to the kid
gloves waiting on the table

of the board meeting for the directors
to put on before beginning
their gang warfare – the dawn with
its one cloud the colour of the carnation

in the chairman's buttonhole, and smells,
myriads of them, spiralling
upward from the sacrifice of
integrity to the clogged nostril of God.

Nuclear

It is not that he can't speak;
who created languages
but God? Nor that he won't;
to say that is to imply
malice. It is just that
he doesn't, or does so at times
when we are not listening, in
ways we have yet to recognise

as speech. We call him the dumb
God with an effrontery beyond
pardon. Whose silence so eloquent
as his? What word so explosive
as that one Palestinian
word with the endlessness of its fall-out?

Praise

I praise you because
you are artist and scientist
in one. When I am somewhat
fearful of your power,
your ability to work miracles
with a set-square, I hear
you murmuring to yourself
in a notation Beethoven
dreamed of but never achieved.
You run off your scales of
rain water and sea water, play
the chords of the morning
and evening light, sculpture
with shadow, join together leaf
by leaf, when spring
comes, the stanzas of
an immense poem. You speak
all languages and none,
answering our most complex
prayers with the simplicity
of a flower, confronting
us, when we would domesticate you
to our uses, with the rioting
viruses under our lens.

Barn Owl

1

Mostly it is a pale
face hovering in the afterdraught
of the spirit, making both ends meet
on a scream. It is the breath
of the churchyard, the forming
of white frost in a believer,
when he would pray; it is soft
feathers camouflaging a machine.

It repeats itself year
after year in its offspring
the staring pupils it teaches
its music to, that is the voice
of God in the darkness cursing himself
fiercely for his lack of love.

2

and there the owl happens
like white frost as
cruel and as silent
and the time on its
blank face is not
now so the dead
have nothing to go
by and are fast
or slow but never punctual
as the alarm is
over their bleached bones
of its night-strangled cry.

Tears

The man weeps
in her lap and the woman
looks at him through tears
of anger, dropping her words

like coins in the cap
of a beggar. If he had
my learning, he would hear
Nietzsche whispering. If I

had his strength – between
such absences they
get away with it, the
women, and are not happy.

They

The new explorers don't go
anywhere and what they discover
we can't see. But they change our lives.

They interpret absence
as presence, measuring it by the movement
of its neighbours. Their world is

an immense place; deep down is as distant
as far out, but is arrived at
in no time. These are the new

linguists, exchanging across closed
borders the currency of their symbols.
Have I been too long on my knees

worrying over the obscurity
of a message? These have their way, too,
other than prayer of breaking that abstruse code.

Phew !

Not caring about it
but keeping on and the going
not good, getting ever further
away, and the perspectives
enormous. Is there a knowledge
not to be known? There is the tree of man
to be climbed; wait for me,
says the body, waving to us
from halfway up. There is a fork
that we come to over
and over, with a choice
to be made that is not
ours, and the worm gnaws
at the root. We lean far out
over ourselves and see the depths
we could fall to. Help me,
the heart cries, but the mind
jeers at it, knowing that nothing
is holy and is where
it comes from and is the distance
that has to be kept open
between its grasp and its reach.

The Way of It

With her fingers she turns paint
into flowers, with her body
flowers into a remembrance
of herself. She is at work
always, mending the garment
of our marriage, foraging
like a bird for something
for us to eat. If there are thorns
in my life, it is she who
will press her breast to them and sing.

Her words, when she would scold,
are too sharp. She is busy
after for hours rubbing smiles
into the wounds. I saw her,
when young, and spread the panoply
of my feathers instinctively
to engage her. She was not deceived,
but accepted me as a girl
will under a thin moon
in love's absence as someone
she could build a home with
for her imagined child.

The Gap

God woke, but the nightmare
did not recede. Word by word
the tower of speech grew.
He looked at it from the air
he reclined on. One word more and
it would be on a level
with him; vocabulary
would have triumphed. He
measured the thin gap
with his mind. No, no, no,
wider than that! But the nearness
persisted. How to live with
the fact, that was the feat
now. How to take his rest
on the edge of a chasm a
word could bridge.
                  He leaned
over and looked in the dictionary
they used. There was the blank still
by his name of the same
order as the territory
between them, the verbal hunger
for the thing in itself. And the darkness
that is a god's blood swelled
in him, and he let it
to make the sign in the space
on the page, that is in all languages
and none; that is the grammarian's
torment and the mystery
at the cell's core, and the equation
that will not come out, and is
the narrowness that we stare
over into the eternal
silence that is the repose of God.

324

Present

I engage with philosophy
in the morning, with the garden
in the afternoon. Evenings I
fish or coming home empty-handed
put on the music of
César Franck. It is enough,
this. I would be the mirror
of a mirror, effortlessly repeating
my reflections. But there is that
one who will not leave me
alone, writing to me
of her fear; and the news from the city
is not good. I am at the switchboard
of the exchanges of the people
of all time, receiving their messages
whether I will or no. Do you
love me? the voices cry.
And there is no answer; there are
only the treaties and take-overs,
and the vision of clasped
hands over the unquiet blood.

The Porch

Do you want to know his name?
It is forgotten. Would you learn
what he was like? He was like
anyone else, a man with ears
and eyes. Be it sufficient
that in a church porch on an evening
in winter, the moon rising, the frost
sharp, he was driven
to his knees and for no reason
he knew. The cold came at him;
his breath was carved angularly
as the tombstones; an owl screamed.

He had no power to pray.
His back turned on the interior
he looked out on a universe
that was without knowledge
of him and kept his place
there for an hour on that lean
threshold, neither outside nor in.

Fishing

Sometimes I go out with the small men
with dark faces and let my line
down quietly into the water, meditating
as they do for hours on end

on the nature and destiny of fish,
of how they are many and other and good
to eat, willing them by a sort of personal
magic to attach themselves to my hook.

The water is deep. Sometimes from far
down invisible messages arrive.
Often it seems it is for more than fish
that we seek; we wait for the

withheld answer to an insoluble
problem. Life is short. The sea starts
where the land ends; its surface
is all flowers, but within are the

grim inmates. The line trembles; mostly,
when we would reel in the catch, there
is nothing to see. The hook gleams, the
smooth face creases in an obscene

grin. But we fish on, and gradually
they accumulate, the bodies, in the torn
light that is about us and the air
echoes to their inaudible screaming.

Groping

Moving away is only to the boundaries
of the self. Better to stay here,
I said, leaving the horizons
clear. The best journey to make
is inward. It is the interior
that calls. Eliot heard it.
Wordsworth turned from the great hills
of the north to the precipice
of his own mind, and let himself
down for the poetry stranded
on the bare ledges.
                            For some
it is all darkness; for me, too,
it is dark. But there are hands
there I can take, voices to hear
solider than the echoes
without. And sometimes a strange light
shines, purer than the moon,
casting no shadow, that is
the halo upon the bones
of the pioneers who died for truth.

In Context

All my life I tried to believe
in the importance of what Thomas
should say now, do next.
                    There was a context
in which I lived; unseen forces
acted upon me, or made their adjustments
in turn. There was a larger pattern
we worked at: they on a big
loom, I with a small needle,
                        drawing the thread
through my mind, colouring it
with my own thought.
                    Yet a power guided
my hand. If an invisible company
waited to see what I would do,
I in my own way asked for
direction, so we should journey together
a little nearer the accomplishment
of the design.
               Impossible dreamer!
All those years the demolition
                   of the identity proceeded.
Fast as the cells constituted
themselves, they were replaced. It was not
I who lived, but life rather
that lived me. There was no developing
structure. There were only the changes
in the metabolism of a body
greater than mine, and the dismantling
by the self of a self it
              could not reassemble.

The Woman

So beautiful – God himself quailed
at her approach: the long body curved
like the horizon. Why had he made
her so? How would it be, she said,
leaning towards him, if, instead of
quarrelling over it, we divided it
between us? You can have all the credit
for its invention, if you will leave the ordering
of it to me. He looked into her
eyes and saw far down the bones
of the generations that would navigate
by those great stars, but the pull of it
was too much. Yes, he thought, give me their minds'
tribute, and what they do with their bodies
is not my concern. He put his hand in his side
and drew out the thorn for the letting
of the ordained blood and touched her with
it. Go, he said. They shall come to you for ever
with their desire, and you shall bleed for them in return.

At It

I think he sits at that strange table
of Eddington's, that is not a table
at all, but nodes and molecules
pushing against molecules
and nodes; and he writes there
in invisible handwriting the instructions
the genes follow. I imagine his
face that is more the face
of a clock, and the time told by it
is now, though Greece is referred
to and Egypt and empires
not yet begun.
            And I would have
things to say to this God
at the judgement, storming at him,
as Job stormed, with the eloquence
of the abused heart. But there will be
no judgement other than the verdict
of his calculations, that abstruse
geometry that proceeds eternally
in the silence beyond right and wrong.

Play

Your move I would have
said, but he was not
playing; my game a dilemma
that was without horns.

As though one can sit at table
with God! His mind shines
on the black and the white
squares. We stake our all

on the capture of the one
queen, as though to hold life
to ransom. He, if he plays, plays
unconcernedly among the pawns.

The Truce

That they should not advance
beyond certain limits left –
accidentally? – undefined;
and that compensation be paid
by the other side. Meanwhile the
peasant – There are no peasants
in Wales, he said, holding
his liquor as a gentleman
should not – went up and down
his acre, rejecting the pot
of gold at the rainbow's
end in favour of earthier
values: the subsidies gradually
propagating themselves on the guilt
of an urban class.
                 Strenuous
times! Never all day
did the procession of popular
images through the farm
kitchens cease; it was tiring
watching. Such truce as was
called in the invisible
warfare between bad and
worse was where two half-truths
faced one another over
the body of an exhausted
nation, each one waiting for
the other to be proved wrong.

Night Sky

What they are saying is
that there is life there, too;
that the universe is the size it is
to enable us to catch up.

They have gone on from the human;
that shining is a reflection
of their intelligence. Godhead
is the colonisation by mind

of untenanted space. It is its own
light, a statement beyond language
of conceptual truth. Every night
is a rinsing myself of the darkness

that is in my veins. I let the stars inject me
with fire, silent as it is far,
but certain in its cauterising
of my despair. I am a slow

traveller, but there is more than time
to arrive. Resting in the intervals
of my breathing, I pick up the signals
relayed to me from a periphery I comprehend.

The Small Country

Did I confuse the categories?
Was I blind?
Was I afraid of hubris
in identifying this land
with the kingdom? Those stories
about the far journeys, when it was here
at my door; the object
of my contempt that became
the toad with the jewel in its head!
Was a population so small
enough to be called, too many
to be chosen? I called it
an old man, ignoring the April
message proclaiming: Behold,
I make all things new.

The dinosaurs have gone their way
into the dark. The time-span
of their human counterparts
is shortened; everything
on this shrinking planet favours the survival
of the small people, whose horizons
are large only because they are content to look at them
from their own hills.
                        I grow old,
bending to enter the promised
land that was here all the time,
happy to eat the bread that was baked
in the poets' oven, breaking my speech
from the perennial tree
of my people and holding it in my blind hand.

Henry James

It was the eloquence of the unsaid
thing, the nobility of the deed
not performed. They looked sideways
into each other's eyes, met casually
by intention. It was the significance
of an absence, the deprecation
of what was there, the failure
to prove anything that proved his point.

Richness is in the ability
of poverty to conceal itself.
After the curtains deliberately
kept drawn, his phrases were servants moving
silently about the great house of his prose
letting in sunlight into the empty rooms.

Hesitations

I rubbed it
and the spirit appeared
(of history): What you will,
it said. Die, I said.
But it would not.

Old gods are no good;
they are smaller than
they promise, or else they are large
like mountains, leaning over
the soul to admire themselves.

I put the bone back
in its place and went on
with my journey. History
went at my right side
hungry for the horizon.

Were there towns I came
to? The sky over
them was without expression.
No God there. I would have
passed on, but a music

detained me in one of
blood flowing, where two
people side by side
under the arc lamps
lay, from one to the other.

Bravo!

Oh, I know it and don't
care. I know there is nothing in me
but cells and chromosomes
waiting to beget chromosomes
and cells. You could take me to pieces
and there would be no angel hard
by, wringing its hands over
the demolition of its temple.
I accept I'm predictable,
that of the thousands of choices
open to me the computer can calculate
the one I'll make. There is a woman
I know, who is the catalyst
of my conversions, who is
a mineral to dazzle. She will
grow old and her lovers will not
pardon her for it. I have made
her songs in the laboratory
of my understanding, explosives timed
to go off in the blandness of time's face.

Pre-Cambrian

Here I think of the centuries,
six million of them, they say.
Yesterday a fine rain fell;
today the warmth has brought out the crowds.
After Christ, what? The molecules
are without redemption. My shadow
sunning itself on this stone
remembers the lava. Zeus looked down
on a brave world, but there was
no love there; the architecture
of their temples was less permanent
than these waves. Plato, Aristotle,
all those who furrowed the calmness
of their foreheads are responsible
for the bomb. I am charmed here
by the serenity of the reflections
in the sea's mirror. It is a window
as well. What I need
now is a faith to enable me to out-stare
the grinning faces of the inmates of its asylum,
the failed experiments God put away.

Abercuawg

Abercuawg! Where is it?
Where is Abercuawg, that
place where the cuckoos sing?
I asked the professors.
Lo, here, lo, there: on the banks
of a river they explained
how Cuawg had become Dulas.
There was the mansion, Dolguog,
not far off to confirm them. I
looked at the surface of the water,
but the place that I was seeking
was not reflected therein.
I looked as though through a clear
window at pebbles that were the ruins
of no building, with no birds tolling
among them, as in the towers of the mind.

An absence is how we become surer
of what we want. Abercuawg
is not here now, but there. And
there is the indefinable point,
the incarnation of a concept,
the moment at which a little
becomes a lot. I have listened
to the word 'Branwen' and pictured
the horses and the soil red
with their blood, and the trouble
in Ireland, and have opened
my eyes on a child, sticky
with sweets and snivel. And: 'Not
this,' I have cried. 'This is the name,
not the thing that the name
stands for.' I have no faith
that to put a name to
a thing is to bring it
before one. I am a seeker
in time for that which is
beyond time, that is everywhere
and nowhere; no more before

than after, yet always
about to be; whose duration is
of the mind, but free as
Bergson would say of the mind's
degradation of the eternal.

Dialectic

They spoke to him in Hebrew and he understood
them; in Latin and Italian and
he understood them. Speech palled
on them and they turned to the silence
of their equations. But God listened to them
as to a spider spinning its web
from its entrails, the mind swinging
to and fro over an abysm
of blankness. They are speaking to me still,
he decided, in the geometry
I delight in, in the figures
that beget more figures. I will answer
them as of old with the infinity
I feed on. If there were words once
they could not understand, I will show
them now space that is bounded
but without end, time that is where
they were or will be; the eternity
that is here for me and for them
there; the truth that with much labour
is born with them and is to be
sloughed off like some afterbirth of the spirit.

Shadows

I close my eyes.
The darkness implies your presence,
the shadow of your steep mind
on my world. I shiver in it.
It is not your light that
can blind us; it is the splendour
of your darkness.
                    And so I listen
instead and hear the language
of silence, the sentence
without an end. Is it I, then,
who am being addressed? A God's words
are for their own sake; we hear
at our peril. Many of us have gone
mad in the mastering
of your medium.
                    I will open
my eyes on a world where the problems
remain but our doctrines
protect us. The shadow of the bent cross
is warmer than yours. I see how the sinners
of history run in and out
at its dark doors and are not confounded.

The Signpost

Casgob, it said, 2
miles. But I never went
there; left it like an ornament
on the mind's shelf, covered

with the dust of
its summers; a place on a diet
of the echoes of stopped
bells and children's

voices; white the architecture
of its clouds, stationary
its sunlight. It was best
so. I need a museum

for storing the dream's
brittler particles in. Time
is a main road, eternity
the turning that we don't take.

Adjustments

Never known as anything
but an absence, I dare not name him
as God. Yet the adjustments
are made. There is an unseen
power, whose sphere is the cell
and the electron. We never catch
him at work, but can only say,
coming suddenly upon an amendment,
that here he has been. To demolish
a mountain you move it stone by stone
like the Japanese. To make a new coat
of an old, you add to it gradually
thread by thread, so such change
as occurs is more difficult to detect.

Patiently with invisible structures
he builds, and as patiently
we must pray, surrendering the ordering
of the ingredients to a wisdom that
is beyond our own. We must change the mood
to the passive. Let the deaf men
be helped; in the silence that has come
upon them, let some influence
work so those closed porches
be opened once more. Let the bomb
swerve. Let the raised knife of the murderer
be somehow deflected. There are no
laws there other than the limits of
our understanding. Remembering rock
penetrated by the grass-blade, corrected
by water, we must ask rather
for the transformation of the will
to evil, for more loving
mutations, for the better ventilating
of the atmosphere of the closed mind.

The Game

It is the play of a being
who is not serious in
his conclusions. Take this
from that, he says, and there is everything
left. Look over the edge
of the universe and you see
your own face staring
at you back, as it does
in a pool. And we are forced
into the game, reluctant
contestants; though the mathematicians
are best at it. Never mind, they
say, whether it is there
or not, so long as our like
can use it. And we are shattered
by their deductions. There is
a series that is without
end, yet the rules are built
on the impossibility of
its existence. It is
how you play, we cry, scanning
the future for an account
of our performance. But the rewards
are there even so, and history
festers with the numbers of the recipients
of them, the handsome, the fortunate,
the well-fed; those who cheated this
being when he was not looking.

Waiting

Face to face? Ah, no
God; such language falsifies
the relation. Nor side by side,
nor near you, nor anywhere
in time and space.
              Say you were,
when I came, your name
vouching for you, ubiquitous
in its explanations. The
earth bore and they reaped:
God, they said, looking
in your direction. The wind
changed; over the drowned
body it was you
they spat at.
              Young
I pronounced you. Older
I still do, but seldomer
now, leaning far out
over an immense depth, letting
your name go and waiting,
somewhere between faith and doubt,
for the echoes of its arrival.

Gone?

Will they say on some future
occasion, looking over the flogged acres
of ploughland: This was Prytherch country?
Nothing to show for it now: hedges
uprooted, walls gone, a mobile people
hurrying to and fro on their fast
tractors; a forest of aerials
as though an invading fleet invisibly
had come to anchor among these
financed hills. They copy the image
of themselves projected on their smooth
screens to the accompaniment of inane
music. They give grins and smiles
back in return for the money that is
spent on them. But where is the face
with the crazed eyes that through the unseen
drizzle of its tears looked out
on this land and found no beauty
in it, but accepted it, as a man
will who has needs in him that only
bare ground, black thorns and the sky's
                    emptiness can fulfil?

The Empty Church

They laid this stone trap
for him, enticing him with candles,
as though he would come like some huge moth
out of the darkness to beat there.
Ah, he had burned himself
before in the human flame
and escaped, leaving the reason
torn. He will not come any more

to our lure. Why, then, do I kneel still
striking my prayers on a stone
heart? Is it in hope one
of them will ignite yet and throw
on its illumined walls the shadow
of someone greater than I can understand?

Album

My father is dead.
I who am look at him
who is not, as once he
went looking for me
in the woman who was.

There are pictures
of the two of them, no
need of a third, hand
in hand, hearts willing
to be one but not three.

What does it mean
life? I am here I am
there. Look! Suddenly
the young tool in their hands
for hurting one another.

And the camera says:
Smile; there is no wound
time gives that is not bandaged
by time. And so they do the
three of them at me who weep.

In Great Waters

You are there also
at the foot of the precipice
of water that was too steep
for the drowned: their breath broke
and they fell. You have made an altar
out of the deck of the lost
trawler whose spars
are your cross. The sand crumbles
like bread; the wine is
the light quietly lying
in its own chalice. There is
a sacrament there more beauty
than terror whose ministrant
you are and the aisles are full
of the sea shapes coming to its celebration.

Travels

I travelled, learned new ways
to deceive, smiling not
frowning; kept my lips supple
with lies; learned to digest
malice, knowing it tribute
to my success. Is the world
large? Are there areas uncharted
by the imagination? Never betray
your knowledge of them. Came here,
followed the river upward
to its beginning in the Welsh
moorland, prepared to analyse
its contents; stared at the smooth pupil
of water that stared at me
back as absent-mindedly as a god
in contemplation of his own
navel; felt the coldness
of unplumbed depths I should have
stayed here to fathom; watched the running
away of the resources
of water to form those far
seas that men must endeavour
to navigate on their voyage home.

Perhaps

His intellect was the clear mirror
he looked in and saw the machinery of God
assemble itself? It was one that reflected
the emptiness that was where God
should have been. The mind's tools had
no power convincingly to put him
together. Looking in that mirror was a journey
through hill mist where, the higher
one ascends, the poorer the visibility
becomes. It could have led to despair
but for the consciousness of a presence
behind him, whose breath clouding
that looking-glass proved that it was alive.
To learn to distrust the distrust
of feeling – this then was the next step
for the seeker? To suffer himself to be persuaded
of intentions in being other than the crossing
of a receding boundary which did not exist?
To yield to an unfelt pressure that, irresistible
in itself, had the character of everything
but coercion? To believe, looking up
into invisible eyes shielded against love's
glare, in the ubiquity of a vast concern?

Roger Bacon

He had strange dreams
  that were real
in which he saw God
   showing him an aperture
    of the horizon wherein
  were flasks and test-tubes.
   And the rainbow
ended there not in a pot
  of gold, but in colours
that, dissected, had the ingredients of
  the death ray.

  Faces at the window
   of his mind
  had the false understanding
of flowers, but their eyes pointed
   like arrows to
  an imprisoning cell.
      Yet
  he dreamed on in curves
   and equations
with the smell of saltpetre
in his nostrils, and saw the hole
   in God's side that is the wound
   of knowledge and
thrust his hand in it and believed.

Emerging

Well, I said, better to wait
for him on some peninsula
of the spirit. Surely for one
with patience he will happen by
once in a while. It was the heart
spoke. The mind, sceptical as always
of the anthropomorphisms
of the fancy, knew he must be put together
like a poem or a composition
in music, that what he conforms to
is art. A promontory is a bare
place; no God leans down
out of the air to take the hand
extended to him. The generations have
watched there
in vain. We are beginning to see
now it is matter is the scaffolding
of spirit; that the poem emerges
from morphemes and phonemes; that
as form in sculpture is the prisoner
of the hard rock, so in everyday life
it is the plain facts and natural happenings
that conceal God and reveal him to us
little by little under the mind's tooling.

After Jericho

There is an aggression of fact
to be resisted successfully
only in verse, that fights language
with its own tools. Smile, poet,

among the ruins of a vocabulary
you blew your trumpet against.
It was a conscript army; your words,
every one of them, are volunteers.

Synopsis

Plato offered us little
the Aristotelians did not
take back. Later Spinoza
rationalised our approach;
we were taught that love
is an intellectual mode
of our being. Yet Hume questioned
the very existence of lover
or loved. The self he left us
with was what Kant
failed to transcend or Hegel
to dissolve: that grey subject
of dread that Søren Kierkegaard
depicted crossing its thousands
of fathoms; the beast that rages
through history; that presides smiling
at the councils of the positivists.

The White Tiger

It was beautiful as God
must be beautiful; glacial
eyes that had looked on
violence and come to terms

with it; a body too huge
and majestic for the cage in which
it had been put; up
and down in the shadow

of its own bulk it went,
lifting, as it turned,
the crumpled flower of its face
to look into my own

face without seeing me. It
was the colour of the moonlight
on snow and as quiet
as moonlight, but breathing

as you can imagine that
God breathes within the confines
of our definition of him, agonising
over immensities that will not return.

The Answer

Not darkness but twilight
in which even the best
of minds must make its way
now. And slowly the questions
occur, vague but formidable
for all that. We pass our hands
over their surface like blind
men, feeling for the mechanism
that will swing them aside. They
yield, but only to re-form
as new problems; and one
does not even do that
but towers immovable
before us.
        Is there no way
other than thought of answering
its challenge? There is an anticipation
of it to the point of
dying. There have been times
when, after long on my knees
in a cold chancel, a stone has rolled
from my mind, and I have looked
in and seen the old questions lie
folded and in a place
by themselves, like the piled
graveclothes of love's risen body.

The Film of God

Sound, too? The recorder
that picks up everything picked
up nothing but the natural
background. What language
does the god speak? And the camera's
lens, as sensitive to
an absence as to a presence,
saw what? What is the colour
of his thought?
                    It was blank, then,
the screen, as far as he
was concerned? It was a bare
landscape and harsh, and geological
its time. But the rock was
bright, the illuminated manuscript
of the lichen. And a shadow,
as we watched, fell, as though
of an unseen writer bending over
his work.
                    It was not cloud
because it was not cold,
and dark only from the candlepower
behind it. And we waited
for it to move, silently
as the spool turned, waited
for the figure that cast it
to come into view for us to
identify it, and it
didn't and we are still waiting.

The Absence

It is this great absence
that is like a presence, that compels
me to address it without hope
of a reply. It is a room I enter

from which someone has just
gone, the vestibule for the arrival
of one who has not yet come.
I modernise the anachronism

of my language, but he is no more here
than before. Genes and molecules
have no more power to call
him up than the incense of the Hebrews

at their altars. My equations fail
as my words do. What resource have I
other than the emptiness without him of my whole
being, a vacuum he may not abhor?

Balance

No piracy, but there is a plank
to walk over seventy thousand fathoms,
as Kierkegaard would say, and far out
from the land. I have abandoned
my theories, the easier certainties
of belief. There are no handrails to
grasp. I stand and on either side
there is the haggard gallery
of the dead, those who in their day
walked here and fell. Above and
beyond there is the galaxies'
violence, the meaningless wastage
of force, the chaos the blond
hero's leap over my head
brings him nearer to.
                 Is there a place
here for the spirit? Is there time
on this brief platform for anything
other than mind's failure to explain itself?

Epiphany

Three kings? Not even one
any more. Royalty
has gone to ground, its journeyings
over. Who now will bring

gifts and to what place? In
the manger there are only the toys
and the tinsel. The child
has become a man. Far

off from his cross in the wrong
season he sits at table
with us with on his head
the fool's cap of our paper money.

Pilgrimages

There is an island there is no going
to but in a small boat the way
the saints went, travelling the gallery
of the frightened faces of
the long-drowned, munching the gravel
of its beaches. So I have gone
up the salt lane to the building
with the stone altar and the candles
gone out, and kneeled and lifted
my eyes to the furious gargoyle
of the owl that is like a god
gone small and resentful. There
is no body in the stained window
of the sky now. Am I too late?
Were they too late also, those
first pilgrims? He is such a fast
God, always before us and
leaving as we arrive.

                            There are those here
not given to prayer, whose office
is the blank sea that they say daily.
What they listen to is not
hymns but the slow chemistry of the soil
that turns saints' bones to dust,
dust to an irritant of the nostril.

There is no time on this island.
The swinging pendulum of the tide
has no clock; the events
are dateless. These people are not
late or soon; they are just
here with only the one question
to ask, which life answers
by being in them. It is I
who ask. Was the pilgrimage
I made to come to my own
self, to learn that in times
like these and for one like me
God will never be plain and
out there, but dark rather and
inexplicable, as though he were in here?

Jongkind

The Beach at Sainte-Adresse

An agreement between
land and sea, with both using
the same tone? But the boat,
motionless in the sand, refuses

to endorse it, remembering
the fury of the clawing
of white hands. However skilfully
the blue surface mirrors

the sky, to the boat it is
the glass lid of a coffin
within which by cold lips
the wooden carcases are mumbled.

Monet

Portrait of Madame Gaudibert

Waiting for the curtain
to rise on an audience
    of one – her husband
who, knowledgeable about ships,
knew how to salvage
    the ship-wrecked painter.

    Comforting
to think how, for a moment
at least, Monet on even
keel paddled himself
on with strokes not
        of an oar but
    of a fast-dipping brush.

Manet

The Balcony

We watch them. They watch
what? The world passes,
they remain, looking
as they were meant to do

at a spectacle
beyond us. It affects them
in several ways. One stares
as at her fortune,

being told. One's hands
are together as if
in applause. The monsieur surmounts
them in sartorial calm.

Degas

The Dancing Class

Pretending he keeps
an aviary; looking no higher
than their feet; listening
for their precise fluttering.

And they surround him, flightless
birds in taffeta
plumage, picking up words
gratefully, as though they were crumbs.

Cézanne

The Card Players

And neither of them has said:
    Your lead.
        An absence of trumps
will arrest movement.

      Knees almost touching,
    hands almost touching,
        they are far away
in time in a world
      of equations.

      The pipe without
    smoke, the empty
    bottle, the light
on the wall are the clock
    they go by.
      Only their minds
      lazily as flies
        drift
round and round the inane
problem their boredom
      has led them to pose.

Degas

Women Ironing

one hand
       on cheek the other
on the bottle
       mouth open
her neighbour
       with hands clasped
not in prayer
       her head bent
over her decreasing
       function   this is art
overcoming permanently
       the temptation to answer
a yawn with a yawn

Van Gogh

Portrait of Dr Gachet

Not part of the Health Service;
no one to pass his failures
on to. The eyes like quinine
have the same medicative

power. With one hand
on cheek, the other
on the equivocal
foxglove he listens

to life as it describes
its symptoms, a doctor
becoming patient himself
of art's diagnosis.

Toulouse-Lautrec

Justine Dieuhl

As we would always wish
    to find her waiting for us,
seated, delphinium-eyed, dressed
for the occasion; out of doors
    since it is always warm
where she is.
           The red kerchief
at the neck, that suggests
blood, is art leading
    modesty astray.
           The hands,
large enough for encircling
the waist's stem, are,
    as ours should be, in
perfect repose, not accessory
to the plucking of her own flower.

Gauguin

Breton Village in the Snow

This is the village
    to which the lost traveller
came, searching for his first spring,
    and found, lying asleep
in the young snow, how cold
    was its blossom.
                The trees
are of iron, but nothing
    is forged on them. The tower
is a finger pointing
    up, but at whom?
                If prayers
are said here, they are
    for a hand to roll
back this white quilt
    and uncover the bed
where the earth is asleep,
    too, but nearer awaking.

Directions

In this desert of language
    we find ourselves in,
with the sign-post with the word 'God'
    worn away
        and the distance ...?

Pity the simpleton
    with his mouth open crying:
        How far is it to God?

And the wiseacre says: Where you were,
friend.
    You know that smile
        glossy
as the machine that thinks it has outpaced
    belief?
        I am one of those
who sees from the arms opened
        to embrace the future
the shadow of the Cross fall
    on the smoothest of surfaces
        causing me to stumble.

Covenant

I feel sometimes
    we are his penance
for having made us. He
suffers in us and we partake
    of his suffering. What
to do, when it has been done
    already ? Where
    to go, when the arrival
is as the departure ? Circularity
is a mental condition, the
animals know nothing of it.

    Seven times have passed
over him, and he is still here.
    When will he return
from his human exile, and will
peace then be restored
    to the flesh ?
                Often
I think that there is no end
to this torment and that the electricity
that convulses us is the fire
    in which a god
burns and is not consumed.

Waiting

Yeats said that. Young
I delighted in it:
there was time enough.

Fingers burned, heart
seared, a bad taste
in the mouth, I read him

again, but without trust
any more. What counsel
has the pen's rhetoric

to impart? Break mirrors, stare
ghosts in the face, try
walking without crutches

at the grave's edge? Now
in the small hours
of belief the one eloquence

to master is that
of the bowed head, the bent
knee, waiting, as at the end

of a hard winter
for one flower to open
on the mind's tree of thorns.

Saraband

That was before the Revolution
as it must always be for the heart
to appraise it. I think they met
in the peculiar sultriness
of August ... And the voice says: Carry
on; I am interested. But I labour
to find my way. It is true
that I made my choice and the poem
cannot hit back; but the colour of it
is not that which her eyes made,
cold stones in the fierce river
of his breath, while the lark's clockwork
went on and on.
                    What a wild country
it is, as hot and dry for one part
of the year, as it is dead and cold
for the other; and the frost comes down
like a great bird, hovering silently
over the homes of an inert people
who have never known either freedom or love.

Correspondence

You ask why I don't write.
But what is there to say?
The salt current swings in and out
of the bay, as it has done
time out of mind. How does that help?
It leaves illegible writing
on the shore. If you were here,
we would quarrel about it.
People file past this seascape
as ignorantly as through a gallery
of great art. I keep searching for meaning.
The waves are a moving staircase
to climb, but in thought only.
The fall from the top is as sheer
as ever. Younger I deemed truth
was to come at beyond the horizon.
Older I stay still and am
as far off as before. These nail-parings
bore you? They explain my silence.
I wish there were as simple
an explanation for the silence of God.

Pluperfect

It was because there was nothing to do
that I did it; because silence was golden
I broke it. There was a vacuum
I found myself in, full of echoes
of dead languages. Where to turn
when there are no corners? In curved
space I kept on arriving
at my departures. I left no stones
unraised, but always wings
were tardy to start. In ante-rooms
of the spirit I suffered the anaesthetic
of time and came to with my hurt
unmended. Where are you? I
shouted, growing old in
the interval between here and now.

Fair Day

They come in from the fields
with the dew and the buttercup dust
on their boots. It was not they
nor their ancestors crucified
Christ. They look up at what
the town has done to him,
hanging his body in stone on a stone
cross, as though to commemorate
the bringing of the divine beast
to bay and disabling him.

He is hung up high, but higher
are the cranes and scaffolding
of the future. And they stand by,
men from the past, whose rôle
is to assist in the destruction
of the past, bringing their own beasts
in to offer their blood up
on a shoddier altar.
                        The town
is malignant. It grows, and what
it feeds on is what these men call
their home. Is there praise
here? There is the noise of those
buying and selling and mortgaging
their conscience, while the stone
eyes look down tearlessly. There
is not even anger in them any more.

Voices

Who to believe?
The linnet sings bell-like,
a tinkling music. It says life
is contained here; is a jewel

in a shell casket, lying
among down. There is another
voice, far out in space,
whose persuasiveness is the distance

from which it speaks. Divided
mind, the message is always
in two parts. Must it be
on a cross it is made one?

Arriving

A maze, he said,
    and at the centre
    the Minotaur
        awaits us.

There are turnings
    that are no through road
    to the fearful.
        By one I came

travelling it
    like a gallery
    of the imagination,
        pausing to look

at the invisible portraits
    of brave men.
    Their deeds rustled
        like dry leaves

under my tread.
    The scent of them was
    the dust we throw
        in the eyes of the beast.

Aleph

What is time? The man stands
in the grass under
the willow by the grey
water corrugated
by wind, and his spirit reminds
him of how it was always
so, in Athens, in Sumer under
the great king. The moment
is history's navel
and round it the worlds
spin. Was there desire
in the past? It is fulfilled
here. The mind has emerged
from the long cave without
looking back, leading eternity
by the hand, and together they pause
on the adult threshold
recuperating endlessly
in intermissions of the machine.

Seventieth
Birthday

Made of tissue and H$_2$O,
and activated by cells
firing – Ah, heart, the legend
of your person! Did I invent
it, and is it in being still?

In the competition with other
women your victory is assured.
It is time, as Yeats said, is
the caterpillar in the cheek's rose,
the untiring witherer of your petals.

You are drifting away from
me on the whitening current of your hair.
I lean far out from the bone's bough,
knowing the hand I extend
can save nothing of you but your love.

One Way

There was a frontier
I crossed whose passport
was human speech. Looking back
was to silence, to that
wood of hands fumbling
for the unseen thing. I
named it and it was
here. I held out words
to them and they smelled
them. Space gave, time was
eroded. There was one being
would not reply. God,
I whispered, refining
my technique, signalling
to him on the frequencies
I commanded. But always
amid the air's garrulousness
there was the one station
that remained closed.
       Was
there an alternative
medium ? There were some claimed
to be able to call him
down to drink insatiably
at the dark sumps of blood.

Mediterranean

The water is the same;
it is the reflections are different.
Virgil looked in this
mirror. You would not think so.

The lights' jewellery sticks in the throat
of the fish; open
them, you will find a debased
coinage to pay your taxes.

The cicadas sing
on. Looking for them among
the ilex is like trying to translate
a poem into another language.

Senior

At sixty there are still fables
to outgrow, the possessiveness
of language. There is no book
of life with the pen ready
to delete one's name. Judgment
days are the trials we attend
here, whose verdict the future
has no interest in. Is there
a sentence without words?

                                God

is a mode of prayer; cease
speaking and there is only
the silence. Has he his own
media of communication?

What is a galaxy's meaning?
The stars relay to the waste
places of the earth, as they do
to the towns, but it is
a cold message. There is randomness
at the centre, agitation subsisting
at the heart of what would be
endless peace.

                      A man's shadow
falls upon rocks that are
millions of years old, and
thought comes to drink at that dark
pool, but goes away thirsty.

The New Mariner

In the silence
that is his chosen medium
of communication and telling
others about it
in words. Is there no way
not to be the sport
of reason? For me now
there is only the God-space
into which I send out
my probes. I had looked forward
to old age as a time
of quietness, a time to draw
my horizons about me,
to watch memories ripening
in the sunlight of a walled garden.
But there is the void
over my head and the distance
within that the tireless signals
come from. And astronaut
on impossible journeys
to the far side of the self
I return with messages
I cannot decipher, garrulous
about them, worrying the ear
of the passer-by, hot on his way
to the marriage of plain fact with plain fact.

Bent

Heads bowed
    over the entrails,
over the manuscript, the
block, over the rows
        of swedes.

Do they never look up?
    Why should one think
that to be on one's knees
    is to pray?
The aim is to walk tall
        in the sun.
Did the weight of the jaw
    bend their backs,
keeping their vision
    below the horizon?

Two million years
in straightening them
    out, and they are still bent
over the charts, the instruments,
        the drawing-board,
the mathematical navel
    that is the wink of God.

Flowers

But behind the flower
is that other flower
which is ageless, the idea
of the flower, the one
we smell when we imagine
it, that as often
as it is picked blossoms
again, that has the perfection
of all flowers, the purity
without the fragility.
                              Was it
a part of the plan
for humanity to have
flowers about it? They are many
and beautiful, with faces
that are a reminder of those
of our own children, though they come painlessly
from the bulb's womb. We trouble
them as we go by, so they hang
their heads at our unreal
progress.
                   If flowers had minds,
would they not think they were the colour
eternity is, a window that gives
on a still view the hurrying
people must come to and stare at and pass by?

The Presence

I pray and incur
silence. Some take that silence
for refusal.
          I feel the power
that, invisible, catches me
by the sleeve, nudging
          towards the long shelf
that has the book on it I will take down
          and read and find the antidote
to an ailment.
          I know its ways with me;
how it enters my life,
          is present rather
before I perceive it, sunlight quivering
on a bare wall.
          Is it consciousness trying
to get through?
          Am I under
regard?
          It takes me seconds
to focus, by which time
          it has shifted its gaze,
looking a little to one
          side, as though I were not here.

It has the universe
          to be abroad in.
There is nothing I can do
but fill myself with my own
          silence, hoping it will approach
          like a wild creature to drink
there, or perhaps like Narcissus
to linger a moment over its transparent face.

Forest Dwellers

Men who have hardly uncurled
from their posture in the
womb. Naked. Heads bowed, not
in prayer, but in contemplation
of the earth they came from,
that suckled them on the brown
milk that builds bone not brain.

Who called them forth to walk
in the green light, their thoughts
on darkness? Their women,
who are not Madonnas, have babes
at the breast with the wise,
time-ridden faces of the Christ
child in a painting by a Florentine

master. The warriors prepare poison
with love's care for the Sebastians
of their arrows. They have no
God, but follow the contradictions
of a ritual that says
life must die that life
may go on. They wear flowers in their hair.

Return

Taking the next train
to the city, yet always returning
to his place on a bridge
over a river, throbbing

with trout, whose widening
circles are the mandala
for contentment. So will a poet
return to the work laid

on one side and abandoned
for the voices summoning him
to the wrong tasks. Art
is not life. It is not the river

carrying us away, but the motionless
image of itself on a fast-
running surface with which life
tries constantly to keep up.

Salt

The centuries were without
his like; then suddenly
he was there, fishing
in a hurrying river,
the Teifi. But what he caught
were ideas; the water
described a direction;
his thoughts were toy boats
that grew big; one
he embarked on: Suez,
the Far East – the atlas
became familiar
to him as a back-yard.

'Spittle and phlegm!
Listen, sailor,
to the wind piping
in the thin rigging;
go climbing there
to the empty nest
of the black crow. Far
is the deck and farther
your courage.'
                            'Captain,
captain, long
is the wind's tongue
and cold your porridge.
Look up now
and dry your beard;
teach me to ride
in my high saddle
the mare of the sea.'

He fell.
Was it the fall
of the soul
from favour? Past four
decks, and his bones
splintered. Seventeen weeks
on his back. No Welsh,

no English; but the hands
of the Romanians
kind. He became
their mouth-piece, publishing
his rebirth. In a new
body he sailed
away on his old course.

On brisk evenings
before the Trades
the sails named
themselves; he repeated
the lesson. The First
Mate had a hard boot.

Cassiopeia, Sirius,
all the stars
over him, yet none of them
with a Welsh sound.
But the capstan spoke
in *cynghanedd*; from
breaker to breaker
he neared home.

'Evening, sailor.' Red
lips and a tilted smile;
the ports garlanded
with faces. Was he aware
of a vicarage garden
that was the cramped harbour
he came to?
                        Later
the letters began: 'Dear –'
the small pen
in the stubbed hand –
'in these dark waters
the memory of you
is like a –' words scratched
out that would win a smile
from the reader. The deep
sea and the old call
to abandon it

for the narrow channel
from her and back. The chair
was waiting and the slippers
by the soft fire
that would destroy him.

'The hard love I had at her small breasts;
the tight fists that pummelled me;
the thin mouth with its teeth clenched
on a memory.' Are all women
like this? He said so, that man,
my father, who had tasted their lips'
vinegar, coughing it up
in harbours he returned to with his tongue
lolling from droughts of the sea.

The voice of my father
in the night with the hunger
of the sea in it and the emptiness
of the sea. While the house founders
in time, I must listen to him
complaining, a ship's captain
with no crew, a navigator
without a port; rejected
by the barrenness of his wife's
coasts, by the wind's bitterness
off her heart. I take his failure
for ensign, flying it
at my bedpost, where my own
children cry to be born.

Suddenly he was old
in a silence unhaunted
by the wailing signals;

and was put ashore
on that four-walled
island to which all sailors must come.

So he went gleaning
in the flickering stubble,
where formerly his keel reaped.

And the remembered stars
swarmed for him; and the birds, too,
most of them with wrong names.

Always he looked aft
from the chair's bridge, and his hearers
suffered the anachronism of his view.

The form of his
life; the weak smile;
the fingers filed down
by canvas; the hopes
blunted; the lack of understanding
of life creasing the brow
with wrinkles, as though he pondered
on deep things.
                            Out of touch
with the times, landlocked
in his ears' calm, he remembered
and talked; spoiling himself
with his mirth; running the joke
down; giving his orders
again in hospital with his crew
gone. What was a sailor
good for who had sailed
all seas and learned wisdom
from none, fetched up there
in the shallows with his mind's
valueless cargo?

Strange grace, sailor, docked now
in six feet of thick soil,
with the light dribbling on you
from the lamps in a street
of a town you had no love
for. The place is a harbour
for stone sails, and under
it you lie with the becalmed
fleet heavy upon you. This
was never the destination
you dreamed of in that other
churchyard by Teifi.

                    And I,
can I accept your voyages
are done; that there is no tide
high enough to float you off
this mean shoal of plastic
and trash? Six feet down,
and the bone's anchor too
heavy for your child spirit
to haul on and be up and away?

Plas Difancoll

1

Trees, of course, silent attendants,
though no more silent than footmen
at the great table, ministering shadows
waiting only to be ignored.

Leaves of glass, full of the year's
wine, broken repeatedly and
as repeatedly replaced.
A garden ventilated by cool

fountains. Two huge lions
of stone, rampant at the drive
gates, intimidating no one
but those lately arrived

and wondering whether they are too early.
Between hillsides the large house,
classical and out of place
in the landscape, as Welsh as

it is unpronounceable. He
and she, magnificent both, not least
in the confidence of their ignorance
of the insubordination of the future.

2

Down to two servants now and those
grown cheeky; unvisited any more

by the county. The rust of autumn
outside on the landscape and inside in the joints

of these hangers-on. Time running out
for them here in the broken hour-glass

that they live in with its cracked
windows mirroring a consumptive moon.

The fish starve in their waters or
are pilfered from them by the unpunished
    trespassers

from away. The place leans on itself,
sags. There is a conspiracy of the ivy

to bring it down, with no prayers
going up from the meeting-house for its salvation.

3

The owls' home and the starlings',
with moss bandaging its deep wounds
to no purpose, for the wind festers in
them and the light diagnoses
impartially the hopelessness
of its condition. Colonialism
is a lost cause. Yet the Welsh
are here, picknicking among the ruins
on their Corona and potato
crisps, speaking their language without pride,
but with no backward look over the shoulder.

Perspectives

Primeval
Beasts rearing from green slime –
an illiterate country, unable to read
its own name. Stones moved into position
on the hills' sides; snakes laid their eggs
in their cold shadow. The earth suffered
the sky's shrapnel, bled yellow
into the enraged sea. At night heavily
over the heaving forests the moon
sagged. The ancestors of the tigers
brightened their claws. Such sounds
as there were came from the strong
torn by the stronger. The dawn tilted
an unpolished mirror for the runt mind
to look at itself in without recognition.

Neolithic
I shall not be here,
and the way things are going
now won't want to be.
Wheels go no faster
than what pulls them. That land
visible over the sea
in clear weather, they say
we will get there some time
soon and take possession
of it. What then? More acres
to cultivate and no markets
for the crops.
        The young
are not what they were,
smirking at the auspices
of the entrails. Some think
there will be a revival.
I don't believe it. This
plucked music has come
to stay. The natural breathing
of the pipes was to
a different god. Imagine

401

depending on the intestines
of a polecat for accompaniment
to one's worship! I have
attended at the sacrifice
of the language that is the liturgy
the priests like, and felt
the draught that was God
leaving. I think some day
there will be nothing left
but to go back to the place
I came from and wrap
myself in the memory
of how I was young
once and under the covenant
of that God not given to folly.

Christian
They were bearded
like the sea they came
from; rang stone bells
for their stone hearers.

Their cells fitted them
like a coffin.
Out of them their prayers
seeped, delicate

flowers where weeds
grew. Their dry bread
broke like a bone.
Wine in the cup

was a blood-stained mirror
for sinners to look
into with one eye
closed, and see themselves forgiven.

Mediaeval
I was my lord's bard,
telling again sweetly
what had been done bloodily.

We lived in a valley;
he had no lady.
Fame was our horizon.

In the spring of the year
the wind brought the news
of a woman's beauty.

Her eyes were still stones
in her smooth-running hair.
Her voice was the birds' envy.

We made a brave foray;
the engagement was furious.
We came back alone.

Sing me, my lord said,
the things nearer home:
my falcons, my horse.

I did so, he listened.
My harp was of fire;
the notes bounced like sparks

off his spirit's anvil.
Tomorrow, he promised,
we will ride forth again.

Modern
And the brittle gardens
of Dinorwig, deep
in the fallen petals of
their slate flowers: such the autumn

of a people! Whose spring
is it sleeps in a glass
bulb, ready to astonish us
with its brilliance? Bring

on the dancing girls
of the future, the swaying
pylons with their metal
hair bickering towards England.

Covenanters

Jesus
He wore no hat, but he produced, say
from up his sleeve, an answer
to their question about
the next life. It is here,
he said, tapping his forehead
as one would to indicate
an idiot. The crowd frowned

and took up stones
to punish his adultery
with the truth. But he, stooping
to write on the ground, looked
sideways at them, as they withdrew
each to the glass-house of his own mind.

Mary
Model of models;
virgin smile over
the ageless babe,

my portrait is in
the world's galleries:
motherhood without

a husband; chastity
my complexion. Cradle
of flesh for one

not born of the flesh.
Alas, you painters
of a half-truth, the

poets excel you.
They looked in under
my lids and saw

404

as through a stained glass
window the hill
the infant must climb,

the crookedness of
the kiss he appended
to his loving epistle.

Joseph
I knew what I knew.
She denied it.
I went with her
on the long journey.
My seed was my own
seed, was the star
that the wise men
followed. Their gifts were no good
to us. I taught him
the true trade : to go
with the grain.
                    He left me
for a new master
who put him to the fashioning
of a cross for himself.

Lazarus
That imperious summons! Spring's
restlessness among dry
leaves. He stands at the grave's
entrance and rubs death from his eyes,

while thought's fountain recommences
its play, watering the waste ground
over again for the germination
of the blood's seed, where roses should blow.

Judas Iscariot
picked flowers stole birds' eggs
like the rest was his mother's
fondling passed under the tree
he would hang from without
realising looked through the branches

saw only the cloud face
of God and the sky mirroring
the water he was brought up by

was a shrewd youth with a talent
for sums became treasurer
to the disciples was genuinely
hurt by a certain extravagance
in the Master went out of his own
free will to do that which he had to do.

Paul
Wrong question, Paul. Who am I,
Lord? is what you should have asked.
And the answer, surely, somebody
who it is easy for us to kick against.
There were some matters you were dead right
about. For instance, I like you
on love. But marriage – I would have thought
too many had been burned in that fire
for your contrast to hold.
                    Still, you are the mountain
the teaching of the carpenter of Nazareth
congealed into. The theologians
have walked round you for centuries
and none of them scaled you. Your letters remain
unanswered, but survive the recipients
of them. And we, pottering among the foot-hills
of their logic, find ourselves staring
across deep crevices at conclusions at which
the living Jesus would not willingly have arrived.

Thirteen Blackbirds Look at a Man ❧

1

It is calm.
It is as though
we lived in a garden
that had not yet arrived
at the knowledge of
good and evil.
But there is a man in it.

2

There will be
rain falling vertically
from an indifferent
sky. There will stare out
from behind its
bars the face of the man
who is not enjoying it.

3

Nothing higher
than a blackberry
bush. As the sun comes up
fresh, what is the darkness
stretching from horizon
to horizon? It is the shadow
here of the forked man.

4

We have eaten
the blackberries and spat out
the seeds, but they lie
glittering like the eyes of a man.

5

After we have stopped
singing, the garden is disturbed
by echoes; it is
the man whistling, expecting
everything to come to him.

6

We wipe our beaks
on the branches
wasting the dawn's
jewellery to get rid
of the taste of a man.

7

Nevertheless,
which is not the case
with a man, our
bills give us no trouble.

8

Who said the
number was unlucky?
It was the man, who,
trying to pass us,
had his licence endorsed
thirteen times.

9

In the cool
of the day the garden
seems given over
to blackbirds. Yet
we know also that somewhere
there is a man in hiding.

10

To us there are
eggs and there are
blackbirds. But there is the man,
too, trying without feathers
to incubate a solution.

11

We spread our
wings, reticulating
our air-space. A man stands
under us and worries
at his ability to do the same.

12

When night comes
like a visitor
from outer space
we stop our ears
lest we should hear tell
of the man in the moon.

13

Summer is
at an end. The migrants
depart. When they return
in spring to the garden,
will there be a man among them?

The Other

They did it to me.
I preferred dead, lying
in the mind's mortuary.
Come out, they shouted;
with a screech of steel
I jumped into the world
smiling my cogged smile,
breaking with iron hand
the hands they extended.

They rose in revolt;
I cropped them like tall
grass; munched on the cud
of nations. A little oil,
I begged in conspiracy
with disaster. Ice
in your veins, the poet
taunted; the life in you
ticking away; your breath
poison. I took him apart
verse by verse, turning
on him my x-ray
eyes to expose the emptiness
of his interiors. In houses
with no hearth he huddles
against me now, mortgaging
his dwindling techniques
for the amenities I offer.

Gradual

I have come to the borders
of the understanding. Instruct
me, God, whether to press
onward or to draw back.

To say I am a child
is a pretence at humility
that is unworthy of me.
Rather am I at one with those

minds, all of whose instruments
are beside the point of
their sharpness. I need a technique
other than that of physics

for registering the ubiquity
of your presence. A myriad prayers
are addressed to you in a thousand
languages and you decode

them all. Liberty for you
is freedom from our too human
senses, yet we die
when they nod. Call your horizons

in. Suffer the domestication
for a moment of the ferocities
you inhabit, a garden for us to refine
our ignorance in under the boughs of love.

Measure for Measure

In every corner
      of the dark triangle
sex spins its web; the characters
are ensnared; virtue
is its own undoing, lust posing
      as love. Life's innocent
need of itself is the prime sin.

And no one able to explain why
at the margins of her habit
the fifteenth phase of the flesh
      so mercilessly dazzles.

The Cones

But why a thousand? I ask.
It is like breaking off
a flake from the great pyramid
of time and exalting the molecules
into wholes. The pyramid
is the hive to which
generation after generation
comes with nectar for the making
of the honey it shall not eat.
Emperors and their queens? Pollen
blown away from forgotten
flowers. Wars? Scratches upon earth's
ageless face. He leads us to expect
too much. Following his star,
we will find in the manger
as the millennium dies neither
the child reborn nor the execrable
monster, but only the curled-up
doll, whose spring is the tribute
we bring it, that before we have done
rubbing our eyes will be back
once more in the arms of the maternal
grass in travesty of the Pietà.

Adder

What is this creature discarded
like a toy necklace
among the weeds and flowers,
singing to me silently

of the fire never to be put out
at its thin lips? It is scion
of a mighty ancestor
that spoke the language

of trees to our first
parents and greened its scales
in the forbidden one, timelessly shining
as though autumn were never to be.

Cadenza

Is absence enough?
I asked from my absent place
by love's fire. What god,
fingers in its ears, leered at me
from above the lintel, face
worn by the lapping
of too much time? Leaves prompted
to prayer, green hands folded
in green evenings. Who
to? I questioned, avoiding
that chipped gaze. Was lightning
the answer, scissoring
between clouds, the divine
cut-out with his veins
on fire? That such brightness
should be attended by such
noise! I supposed, watching
the starry equations,
his thinking was done
in a great silence; yet after
he goes out, following
himself into oblivion,
the memory of him must smoke
on in this ash, waiting
for the believing people
to blow on it. So some say
were the stars born. So,
say I, are those sparks
forged that are knocked like nails
one by one into the usurping flesh.

Centuries

The fifteenth passes with drums and in armour;
the monk watches it through the mind's grating.

The sixteenth puts on its cap and bells
to poach vocabulary from a king's laughter.

The seventeenth wears a collar of lace
at its neck, the flesh running from thought's candle.

The eighteenth has a high fever and hot blood,
but clears its nostrils with the snuff of wit.

The nineteenth emerges from history's cave
rubbing its eyes at the glass prospect.

The twentieth is what it looked forward to
beating its wings at windows that are not there.

The Tree

So God is born
        from our loss of nerve?
He is the tree that looms up
in our darkness, at whose feet
we must fall to be set again
on its branches on some April day
of the heart.
                He needs us
as a conductor his choir
for the performance of an unending
music.
              What we may not
do is to have our horizon bare,
           is to make our way
on through a desert white with the bones
of our dead faiths. It is why,
some say, if there were no tree,
we would have to set one up
             for us to linger under,
its drops falling on us as though to confirm
he has blood like ourselves.
We have set one up, but
of steel and so leafless that
            he has taken himself
off out of the reach
of our transmitted prayers.
                 Nightly
we explore the universe
on our wave-lengths, picking up nothing
           but those acoustic ghosts
that could as well be mineral
          signalling to mineral
as immortal mind communicating with itself.

Grandparents

With the deterioration of sight
they see more clearly what is missing
from their expressions. With the
dulling of the ear, the silences
before the endearments are
louder than ever. Their hands have their accidents
still, but no hospital will
receive them. With their licences
expired, though they keep to their own
side, there are corners
in waiting. Theirs is a strange
house. Over the door in
invisible letters there is the name:
Home, but it is no place
to return to. On the floor
are the upset smiles, on the
table the cups unwashed they drank
their happiness from. There are themselves
at the windows, faces staring
at an unreached finishing
post. There is the sound
in the silence of the breathing
of their reluctant bodies as
they enter each of them the last lap.

Publicity Inc.

Homo sapiens to the Creator:
Greetings, on the mind's kiloherz.
For yours of no date,
thanks. This is to advise
that as of now our address
broadens to include the planets
and the intervals between. No
longer the old gravitational
pull. We are as much
out there as down here. As likely
to meet you on the way back
as at our departure.
You refer to the fading away
of our prayers. May we suggest
you try listening on the inter-galactic
channel? Realising the sound
returned to us from a flower's
speaking-trumpet was an echo
of our own voices, we have switched
our praise, directing it rather
at those mysterious sources
of the imagination you yourself
drink from, metabolising
them instantly in space-time
to become the ichor of your radiation.

History

It appears before us,
    wringing its dry hands,
quoting from Nietzsche's book,
    from Schopenhauer.

Sing us, we say,
    more sunlit occasions;
the child by the still pool
    multiplying reflections.

It remains unconsoled
    in its dust-storm of tears,
remembering the Crusades,
    the tortures, the purges.

But time passes by;
    it commits adultery
with it to father the cause
    of its continued weeping.

Passage

I was Shakespeare's man that time,
           walking under a waned moon
to hear the barn owl cry:
           Treason. My sword failed me,
              withering at its green
tip.
       I took Donne's word,
clothing my thought's skeleton
         in black lace, walking awhile
           by the bone's light;
but the tombstone misled me.

          Shelley put forth
his waxwork hand, that came off
in my own and I sank down
         with him to see time
          as its experiment at the sand's
table.
        I walked Yeats'
street, pausing at the flowering
        of the water in a shop
window, foreseeing its drooping
         from being too often
smelled.
        I stand now, tolling my name
in the poem's empty church,
        summoning to the celebration
         at which the transplanted
organs are loth to arrive.

The Bush

I know that bush,
Moses; there are many of them
in Wales in the autumn, braziers
where the imagination
warms itself. I have put off
pride and, knowing the ground
holy, lingered to wonder
how it is that I do not burn
and yet am consumed.

And in this country
of failure, the rain
falling out of a black
cloud in gold pieces there
are none to gather,
I have thought often
of the fountain of my people
that played beautifully here
once in the sun's light
like a tree undressing.

Contacts

The wheel revolves
          to bring round the hour
for this one to return to the darkness
and be born again on a chill
          doorstep, and have the blood washed
from his eyes and his hands
          made clean for the re-building

of the city. While for this one
          it revolves to make the tanks
          stronger the aeroplanes faster.

The scholar bends over
his book and the sage his navel
          to enter the labyrinthine
mind and find at the centre the axis
on which it spins. But for the one
          who is homeless
there is only the tree with the body
          on it, eternally convulsed
by the shock of its contact
with the exposed nerve of love.

Inside

I am my own
geology, strata on strata
of the imagination, tufa
dreams, the limestone mind
honeycombed by the running away
of too much thought. Examine
me, tap with your words'
hammer, awaken memories
of fire. It is so long
since I cooled. Inside me,
stalactite and stalagmite,
ideas have formed and become
rigid. To the crowd
I am all outside.
To the pot-holing few there is a way
in along passages that become
narrower and narrower,
that lead to the chamber
too low to stand up in,
where the breath condenses
to the cold and locationless
cloud we call truth. It
is where I think.

Island

Of all things to remember
this is special: the Buddha
seated cross-legged, disproving
Donne, himself an island

surrounded by the expanses
of space and time. From his navel
the tree grows whose canopy
is knowledge. He counts the leaves

as they fall, that are words
out of the mouth of the unseen
God, washing his thoughts clean
in them. Over the waters

he sees the argosies of the world
approaching, that will never
arrive, that will go down, each
one sunk by the weight of its own cargo.

Suddenly

Suddenly after long silence
he has become voluble.
He addresses me from a myriad
directions with the fluency
of water, the articulateness
of green leaves; and in the genes,
too, the components
of my existence. The rock,
so long speechless, is the library
of his poetry. He sings to me
in the chain-saw, writes
with the surgeon's hand
on the skin's parchment messages
of healing. The weather
is his mind's turbine
driving the earth's bulk round
and around on its remedial
journey. I have no need
to despair; as at
some second Pentecost
of a Gentile, I listen to the things
round me: weeds, stones, instruments,
the machine itself, all
speaking to me in the vernacular
of the purposes of One who is.

Arrival

Not conscious
    that you have been seeking
        suddenly
    you come upon it

the village in the Welsh hills
    dust free
with no road out
but the one you came in by.

    A bird chimes
from a green tree
the hour that is no hour
    you know. The river dawdles
to hold a mirror for you
where you may see yourself
    as you are, a traveller
        with the moon's halo
    above him, who has arrived
    after long journeying where he
        began, catching this
    one truth by surprise
that there is everything to look forward to.

Brother

It came into being.
From eternity? In
time? Was the womb
prepared for it, or it
for the womb? It lay in the cradle
long months, staring its world
into a shape, decorated
with faces. It addressed
objects, preferred its vocabulary
to their own; grew eloquent
before a resigned
audience. It was fed
speech and vomited
it and was not reproved.
It began walking,
falling, bruising itself
on the bone's truth. The fire
was a tart playmate. It
was taken in by the pool's smile.
Need I go on? It survived
its disasters; met fact
with the mind's guile; forged
for itself wings, missiles.
Launched itself on a dark
night through the nursery
window into adult orbit
out of the reach of gravity's control.

Remembering David Jones

Because you had been in the dark wood
and heard doom's nightingales sing,
men listened to you when you told
them how death is many but life
one. The shell's trumpet sounded
over the fallen, but there was no
resurrection. You learned your lettering
from bones, the propped capitals which described
how once they were human beings.

Men march because they are alive,
and their quest is the Grail, garrisoned
by the old furies so it is blood
wets their lips. Europe gave you
your words, but your hand practised
an earlier language, weaving time's branches
together to form the thicket the soldier
is caught in, who is love's sacrifice
to itself, with the virgin's smile poised
like a knife over it as over her first born.

The Moment

Is the night dark? His interiors
are darker, more perilous
to enter. Are there whispers
abroad? They are the communing

with himself our destiny
is to be outside of, listeners
at our breath's window. Is there
an ingredient in him of unlove?

It is the moment in the mind's
garden he resigns himself
to his own will to conceive the tree
of manhood we have reared against him.

Gospel

And in the midst of the council
a bittern called from the fen
outside. A sparrow flew in
and disappeared through the far doorway.
'If your faith can explain ...' So
they were baptised, and the battles began
for the kingdom of this world. Were
you sent, sparrow? An eagle
would have been more appropriate,
some predator to warn them
of the ferocity of the religion
that came their way. The fire was not more voluble
than the blood that would answer the sword's
question.
       Charles by divine right
king. And not all our engines can drain
Marston Moor. The bittern
is silent now. The ploughshares are beaten
to guns and bombs. Daily we publish
hurrying with it to and fro on steel
wings, the good news of the kingdom.

Minuet

But not to concentrate
on disaster, there are the small
weeds with the caterpillar
at their base that is life's proof
that the beautiful is born
from the demolition of the material.

The butterfly has no
clock. It is always noon
where it is, the sun overhead,
the flower feeding on what feeds
on itself. The wings turn and are sails
of a slow windmill, not to grind
but to be the signal for another
aviator to arrive that the air
may have dancing, a movement
of wings in an invisible
ballroom to a music that,
unheard by ourselves, is to them
as though it will never cease.

Sonata

Evening. The wind rising.
The gathering excitement
of the leaves, and Beethoven
on the piano, chords reverberating
in our twin being.
                                'What is life?'
pitifully her eyes
asked. And I who was no seer
took hold of her loth hand
and examined it and was lost
like a pure mathematician
in its solution: strokes
cancelling strokes; angles
bisected; the line of life deviating
from the line of the head; a way
that was laid down for her to walk
which was not my way.
                                While the music
went on and on with chromatic
insistence, passionately proclaiming
by the keys' moonlight in the darkening
drawing-room how our art is our meaning.

Carol

What is Christmas without
snow ? We need it
as bread of a cold
climate, ermine to trim

our sins with, a brief
sleeve for charity's
scarecrow to wear its heart
on, bold as a robin.

Requiem

To the mature itch I lent my hand;
a sword grew in it, withered
in the exact blood. When next I looked,
murder; the sour commons
attainted me. But the king's head
lapping at the emptying trough
of existence, reprieved me. I took aim
with the long musket, writing in lead
on their horses. Hysterical women
my loot, I rendered complete
service, sowing the blank field again.
Alleluia! The cannonade of the bells
rang. I built a cathedral –
to whom? Decorated it with the stone
population, the dumb mouths, the eyes blinded
by distance. Naughtiness of the chisel
in time's hand distorted the features
of those who had looked on that far
face and lived to bear witness.

Prayer

Baudelaire's grave
not too far
from the tree of science.
Mine, too,
since I sought and failed
to steal from it,
somewhere within sight
of the tree of poetry
that is eternity wearing
the green leaves of time.

Guernica

Pablo Picasso

The day before
        it was calm.
In the days after
        a new masterpiece
was born of imagination's wandering
        of the smashed city.
What but genius can re-assemble
        the bones' jigsaw?
The bull has triumphed
        at last; the tossed
humans descend up-
        side down, never
to arrive. The whole is love
        in reverse. The painter
has been down at the root
        of the scream and surfaced
again to prepare the affections
        for the atrocity of its flowers.

Portrait of a Girl in a Yellow Dress

Henri Matisse

Windows in art
  are to turn the back
on. Facing the public
she challenges it to prefer her
  to the view. The draught
cannot put out
    her flame: yellow
  dress, yellow
    (if we could come close
enough) eyes; hands
  that, after the busyness
of their migrations between cheek
  and dressing-table, lipstick
and lip, have found in the lap's
    taffeta a repose
whose self-consciousness the painter
  was at pains not to conceal.

Father and Child

Ben Shahn

Times change:
no longer the virgin
ample-lapped; the child fallen
in it from an adjacent heaven.

Heaven is far off, back
of the bombed town. The infant
is human, embraced dearly
like a human mistake.

The father presses, his face set,
towards a displaced future.
The mother has salvaged her mother's
portrait and carries it upside down.

Portrait of Madame Renou

André Derain

Could I have loved this?
To show too little
is to ask too much.
A tendency to disdain
our requirements promises
she has nothing to give.
It is not the observer
she pouts at, but life itself.

Yet now the disclosure:
Madame Renou! While the mind
toys with the title, the
rest of me has no time
for the spouse. Art like
this could have left her tagged surname out.

The Good Inn

Frits van den Berghe

Nothing is here
but essentials
the bicycle that conveyed
him his thirst
sharpened by unpalatable
truths and the woman
reaching far down
into unmentionable
depths to draw up
the female alcohol
that will not assuage him.

The Child's Brain

Giorgio di Chirico

The book is as closed
as the mind contemplating
it, vocabulary's
navel in all that gross flesh.

While the school reminds,
windowless at his left
shoulder, how you open
either of them at your own risk.

The Oracle

Giorgio di Chirico

So life in the end
is profane, our worshipping
done in the cemetery
of a blackboard. Who
sits over the bones
of the problem without
face but with certifiable
expression?
                    So mathematicians
should appear in surrealist
mourning, shaven-headed
to reveal the skull
half in darkness, half in light
in permanent procrastination
of the eclipse of thought.

The Red Model

René Magritte

Given the boots
solitary against
the boards, I construct
the body, kneed
and hooded, perforated
with dark, taken
away at dawn on
a barrow to be provender
of a grave.
          Tall
and shapeless, too
(as they deemed)
big for them, he
left them behind,
not for robins
to build nests in,
not for the dust to tell
boneless time; for his out-
at-toe ghost to walk
onward for ever against
an ingrowing thought.

Two Children Menaced
by a Nightingale

Max Ernst

Inviting them into a house
        haunted by a clock
on the wall, whose notes
are its music. The gate
out of the picture by which Keats left
        on his way to eternity
is wide open.
            Fly, children,
        anticipate the nightingale's
        migration. Postpone
the knowledge of the insects
that are required to produce
        its sweetness of tone.
        Remember the babes
in the wood who were discovered
        with their heads buried
in leaves that were the colour
of the feathers of the bird
        that had sung to them,
            pressing sanguinely
        its breast against time.

On the Threshold of Liberty

René Magritte

What it means is:
           you must accede
to the invention. Flesh,
trees, dwellings, the grain
               in the wood
are vulnerable and not
          to be shot at;
only the sky is
        target.
               Challenged
the inventor would claim
        all he wants is
for it to go off.
             So move
the paintings to one side
        in the humanist's
gallery; open a window.
Let the gun point its muzzle,
        silently barking,
at the idea that there are limits.

Captain Cook's Last Voyage

Roland Penrose

Beautiful because
           she is without an arm
to embrace your reasons.

He has thrown the globe
about her and set forth
on his maiden voyage
to the flesh that is the iceberg
           on which we are wrecked.

On eternity's background
           is the shadow
of time's cage, where nautically
           we are becalmed
listening to the echoes
in the nerves' rigging
           of that far-off storm
that is spirit blowing itself
out in the emptiness at the Poles.

Drawing by a Child

Diana Brinton Lee

All of them, Mummy and Daddy
in their various disguises –
   it is my revenge on them
   for bringing me to be.

And, oh, yes! The toys
who play with me, whose justification
   I am. I take my revenge
   on them, too, giving them claws,

indices of the underworld
to which they belong. Can you imagine
   how a doll snarls? With
   what relish a kitten converts

its tail into a serpent?
And horns, horns for everything
   in my nursery, pointing to the
   cuckold I know my father to be.

The Message

A message from God
delivered by a bird
at my window, offering friendship.
Listen. Such language!
Who said God was without
speech? Every word an injection
to make me smile. Meet me,
it says, tomorrow, here
at the same time and you will remember
how wonderful today
was: no pain, no worry;
irrelevant the mystery if
unsolved. I gave you the X-ray
eye for you to use, not
to prospect, but to discover
the unmalignancy of love's
growth. You were a patient, too,
anaesthetised on truth's table,
with life operating on you
with a green scalpel. Meet me, tomorrow,
I say, and I will sing it all over
again for you, when you have come to.

A Poet

Disgust tempered by an exquisite
charity, wrapping life's claws
in purest linen – this man
has history to supper,
eats with a supreme tact
from the courses offered to him.

Waiting at table
are the twin graces, patience
and truth, with the candles'
irises in soft clusters
flowering on thin stalks.

Where did he come from?
Pupating against the time
he was needed, he emerged
with wings furled, unrecognised
by the pundits; has spread
them now elegantly
to dazzle, curtains drawn
with a new nonchalance
between barbarism and ourselves.

Patron without condescension
of the art, he teaches flight's
true purpose, which is,
sensitive but not too blinded
by some inner radiance, to be
in delicatest orbit about it.

The Unvanquished

And courage shall give way
to despair and despair
to suffering, and suffering
shall end in death. But you
who are not free to choose
what you suffer can choose
your response. Farmers I
knew, born to the ills
of their kind, scrubbed bare
by the weather, suffocating
with phlegm; all their means gone
to buy their consumptive son
the profession his body
could not sustain. Proudly
they lived, watching the spirit,
diamond-faceted, crumble
to the small, hard, round, dry
stone that humanity
chokes on. When they died, it
was bravely, close up under the rain-hammered
rafters, never complaining.

Vocabulary

Ruminations, illuminations!
Vocabulary, sing for me
in your cage of time,
restless on the bone's perch.

You are dust; then a bird
with new feathers, but always
beating at the mind's bars.
A new Noah, I despatch

you to alight awhile
on steel branches; then call
you home, looking for the metallic
gleam of a new poem in your bill.

Obstetrics

The sea's skin is smooth.
A part-time surgeon
I make my incision,
and there are born to me
out of its grieved side
cold, glittering bodies
of fishes, the scaled babes
of the sea.
          They lie choking
in air, their eyes focused
on nothing, silently beseeching
with huge, rounded vowels
to be put back.
          There
are plenty more of you,
I think in self-exculpation.
Because of your absence
of mind, your flesh must become
my flesh and parade
under the stars, meditating
upon love with only a memory
of the under-water grottoes.

In Memoriam E. E. T.

Young I offered an old man
friendship. It was not refused.
Leaning from the swaying ladder
up which he had climbed he threw
those few books down that were to be
a memorial of him, when he had withdrawn
into his cloud. I have spent years
winnowing their pages, separating
their philosophy from how he appeared:
the lidless skull; the small hands' mockery
of his ambition in the last war to drive
armoured cars; his angling for connivance
at the helplessness of his merriment
at his own jokes.
              I remember him irrigating
with his German the dried-up consciences
of prisoners; his indulgence
of himself at the piano at Christmas
at lieder's expense. His tales were of duels
among students in the courtyard
of a Leipzig beer-garden; of Harnack
and the mind's reach; of how Lawrence
would answer his critics with ever
a more splendid book.
              I think he has gone
now, looking for the last laugh in Nirvana
or the tearless reflection of it in blond eyes.

Gallery

The stillness of paintings!
Move stealthily so
as not to disturb.

They are not asleep.
They keep watch on
our taste. It is not they

are being looked at
but we by faces
which over the centuries

keep their repose. Such eyes
they have as steadily,
while crowds come and

crowds go, burn on
with art's crocus flame
in their enamelled sockets.

Destinations

Travelling towards the light
we were waylaid by darkness;
a formless company detained us,
saying everything, meaning nothing.

It is a conspiracy, I said,
of great age, in revolt
against reason, against all
that would be ethereal in us.

We looked at one another.
Was it the silence of agreement,
or the vacuum between two minds
not in contact? There is an ingredient

in thought that is its own
hindrance. Had we come all that way
to detect it? The voices combined,
urging us to put our trust

in the bone's wisdom. Remember,
they charged us, the future
for which you are bound is where
you began. Was there a counter

command? I listened as to
a tideless sea on a remote
star, and knew our direction
was elsewhere; to the light, yes,

but not such as minerals
deploy; to the brightness over
an interior horizon, which is science
transfiguring itself in love's mirror.

The Other

There are nights that are so still
that I can hear the small owl calling
far off and a fox barking
miles away. It is then that I lie
in the lean hours awake listening
to the swell born somewhere in the Atlantic
rising and falling, rising and falling
wave on wave on the long shore
by the village, that is without light
and companionless. And the thought comes
of that other being who is awake, too,
letting our prayers break on him,
not like this for a few hours,
but for days, years, for eternity.

The Conviction

There was a face in chapel
with hands folded
over it as though in prayer,
but peering between
fingers at the congregation
to see if it was to the minister
they listened or to itself.

In the intervals in the sermon
there was the insect whispering
of that other commentator
on life, a kind of:
No, no, no, to the affirmatives
of its rival. It was why
they went. If the preacher
was immortal, his homily
was not. There was a moment
towards which it crept
to die at the precise stroke
of the bell. The listeners
rose to their feet and went home
one by one, heretics still
in their conviction that time was God.

He and She

When he came in, she was there.
When she looked at him,
he smiled. There were lights
in time's wave breaking
on an eternal shore.

Seated at table –
no need for the fracture
of the room's silence; noiselessly
they conversed. Thoughts mingling
were lit up, gold
particles in the mind's stream.

Were there currents between them?
Why, when he thought darkly,
would the nerves play
at her lips' brim? What was the heart's depth?
There were fathoms in her,
too, and sometimes he crossed
them and landed and was not repulsed.

Sarn Rhiw

So we know
she must have said something
to him – What language,
life? Ah, what language?

Thousands of years later
I inhabit a house
whose stone is the language
of its builders. Here

by the sea they said little.
But their message to the future
was: Build well. In the fire
of an evening I catch faces

staring at me. In April,
when light quickens and clouds
thin, boneless presences
flit through my room.

Will they inherit me
one day? What certainties
have I to hand on
like the punctuality

with which, at the moon's
rising, the bay breaks
into a smile, as though meaning
were not the difficulty at all?

Mother and Child

No clouds overhead;
no troubles freckling
the maid's eye. The shadows
are immediate and are thrown

by upholstered branches,
not by that angled
event that from beyond
the horizon puts its roots

down. This is Eden
over again. The child
holds out both his hands
for the breast's apple. The snake is asleep.

Siân

Can one make love
to a kitten? Siân,
purr for me; jump
into my lap; knead
me. Shine your claws
in my smile. Your talk is a bell
fastened with ribbon
about your throat. My hand
thrills to the electricity
of your fur. So small
you are, I cradle
you on my arm, wearing
you at my breast-bone. Tune
your pulses to mine.
I know the slits in your eyes
are not to be peeped
through; evidence rather
that you can find your way
through the thick of the darkness
that all too often manages
to invest my heart.

West Coast

Here are men
    who live at the edges
of vast space.
    Light pours on them
and they lift their faces
    to be washed by it
like children. And their minds
    are the minds of children,
shallow pools that the days
    look into, as they
pass in the endless procession
    that goes nowhere.
        They are
    spendthrifts of time, yet
always there is more of it
    than they need for the tongue's clambering
up their one story.
        Out in the fields,
against skies that are all
    blood, they erect the scarecrow
of their kind, the crossed bones
    with the flesh in tatters
upon them that have frightened
    away a lot more than the birds.

Drowning

They were irreplaceable and forgettable,
inhabitants of the parish and speakers
of the Welsh tongue. I looked on and
there was one less and one less and one less.

They were not of the soil, but contributed
to it in dying, a manure not
to be referred to as such, but from which
poetry is grown and legends and green tales.

Their immortality was what they hoped for
by being kind. Their smiles were such as,
exercised so often, became perennial
as flowers, blossoming where they had been cut down.

I ministered uneasily among them until
what had been gaps in the straggling hedgerow
of the nation widened to reveal the emptiness
that was inside, where echoes haunted and thin ghosts.

A rare place, but one identifiable
with other places where on as deep a sea
men have clung to the last spars of their language
and gone down with it, unremembered but uncomplaining.

A Land

Their souls are something smaller
                than the mountain above them
and give them more trouble.
                    They are not touched
either by the sun rising at morning
or the sun setting at evening.
                    They are all in shadow
pale and winding themselves about each other
                    inhibiting growth.

Death lives in this village, the ambulance plies
                    back and fore,
and they look at it through the eternal downpour
                  of their tears.
                    Who was it found
truth's pebble in the stripling
                  river? No one believed him.

They have hard hands that money adheres
                to like the scales
of some hideous disease, so that they grizzle
as it is picked off. And the chapel crouches,
a stone monster, waiting to spring,
waiting with the disinfectant of its language
                  for the bodies rotting with
their unsaid prayers.
                It is at such times
that they sing, not music
                so much as the sound of a nation
rending itself, fierce with all the promise
                  of a beauty that might have been theirs.

Saunders Lewis

And he dared them;
Dared them to grow old and bitter
As he. He kept his pen clean
By burying it in their fat
Flesh. He was ascetic and Wales
His diet. He lived off the harsh fare
Of her troubles, worn yet heady
At moments with the poets' wine.

A recluse, then; himself
His hermitage? Unhabited
He moved among us; would have led
To rebellion. Small as he was
He towered, the trigger of his mind
Cocked, ready to let fly with his scorn.

Dead Worthies

Where is our poetry
but in the footnotes?
What laurels for famous
men but asterisks and numbers?

Branwen (Refer below).
Llywelyn – there is but
one, eternally on his way
to an assignation.

Morgan, no pirate,
emptying his treasure
from buccaneering
among the vocabulary. Ann,

handmaid of the Lord,
giving herself to the
Bridegroom, still virgin.
Williams Parry, quarrying

his cynghanedd among
Bethesda slate in
the twilight of the language.
Lloyd George, not David,

William, who in defence
of what his brother
had abandoned, made a case
out of staying at home.

Waiting

Here are mountains to ascend
not to preach from,
not to summon one's disciples
to, but to see far off the dream that is life:
winged yachts hovering over
a gentian sea; sun-making
windscreens; the human torrent
irrigating tunefully the waste places.

Ah, Jerusalem, Jerusalem!
Is it for nothing our chapels were christened
with Hebrew names? The Book rusts
in the empty pulpits above empty
pews, but the Word ticks inside
remorselessly as the bomb that is timed soon to go off.

Deprivation

All this beauty,
and all the pain
of beholding it emptied
of a people who were not worthy of it.
It is the morning of a world
become suddenly evening.
There was never any noon here.
Noon is an absence of shadow,
the stillness of contemplation,
of a balance achieved
between light and dark.
When they were born,
they began to die to the view
that has been taken from them
by others. Over their sour
tea they talk of a time
they thought they were alive.
God, in this light this
country is a brittle
instrument laid on one side
by one people, taken up
by another to play their twanged
accompaniment upon it, to which
the birds of Rhiannon
are refusing to sing.

Fugue for Ann Griffiths

In which period
    do you get lost?
The roads lead
    under a twentieth century
sky to the peace
    of the nineteenth. There it is,
as she left it,
    too small to be chrysalis
of that clenched soul.
    Under the eaves the martins
continue her singing.
    Down this path she set off
for the earlier dancing
    of the body; but under the myrtle
the Bridegroom was waiting
    for her on her way home.

To put it differently
yet the same, listen,
friend:
    A nineteenth century
            calm;
that is, a countryside
    not fenced in
by cables and pylons,
but open to thought to blow in
    from as near as may be
to the truth.
        There were evenings
she would break it. See her
    at the dance, round
and round, hand
    in hand, weaving
invisible threads. When
you are young ... But
    there was One
with his eye on her;
    she saw him stand
under the branches.

                    History insists
on a marriage, but the husband was as cuckolded
as Joseph.
              Listen again:

      To the knocker at the door:
      'Miss Thomas has gone dancing.'

      To the caller in time:
      'The mistress is sitting the dance

      out with God at her side.'
      To the traveller up learning's

      slope: 'She is ahead of you on her knees.
      She who had decomposed

      is composed again in her hymns.
      The dust settles on the Welsh language,

      but is blown away in great gusts
      week by week in chapel after chapel.'

Is there a scholarship that grows
naturally as the lichen? How
did she, a daughter of the land, come
by her learning? You have seen
her face, figure-head of a ship
outward bound? But she was not
alone; a trinity of persons
saw to it she kept on course
like one apprenticed since early
days to the difficulty of navigation
in rough seas. She described her turbulence
to her confessor, who was the more
astonished at the fathoms
of anguish over which she had
attained to the calmness of her harbours.

      There are other pilgrimages
          to make beside Jerusalem, Rome;
      beside the one into the no-man's-
          land beyond the microscope's carry.

If you came in winter,
    you would find the tree
with your belief still crucified
    upon it, that for her at all

times was in blossom, the resurrection
    of one that had come seminally
down to raise the deciduous human
    body to the condition of his body.

Hostilities were other peoples'.
Though a prisoner of the Lord
she was taken without fighting.

That was in the peace before
the wars that were to end
war. If there was a campaign

for her countrymen, it was one
against sin. Musically
they were conscripted to proclaim

Sunday after Sunday the year
round they were on God's side. England
meanwhile detected its enemies

from afar. These made friends
out in the fields because
of its halo with the ancestral scarecrow.

Has she waited all these years
for me to forget myself
and do her homage? I begin
now: Ann Thomas, Ann Griffiths,
one of a thousand Anns chosen
to confound your parentage
with your culture – I know
Powys, the leafy backwaters
it is easy for the spirit to forget
its destiny in and put on soil
for its crown. You walked solitary
there and were not tempted,

or took your temptation as calling
to see Christ rising in April
out of that same soil and clothing
his nakedness like a tree. Your similes
were agricultural and profound.
As winter is forgiven by spring's
blossom, so defoliated man,
thrusting his sick hand in the earth's
side is redeemed by conviction.
Ann, dear, what can our scholarship
do but wander like Efyrnwy
your grass library, wondering at the absence
of all volumes but one? The question
teases us like the undying
echo of an Amen high up
in the cumulus rafters over Dolanog.

    The theologians disagree
    on their priorities. For her
    the centuries' rhetoric contracted
    to the three-letter word. What was sin
    but the felix culpa enabling
    a daughter of the soil to move
    in divine circles? This was before
    the bomb, before the annihilation
    of six million Jews. It appears now
    the confession of a child before
    an upholstered knee; her achievement
    the sensitising of the Welsh
    conscience to the English rebuke.
    The contemporary miracle is the feeding
    of the multitude on the sublime
    mushroom, while the Jesus,
    who was her lover, is a face
    gathering moss on the gable
    of a defunct chapel, a myth shifting
    its place to the wrong end
    of the spectrum under the Doppler
    effect of the recession of our belief.

Three pilgrimages to Bardsey
equalling one to Rome – How close

need a shrine be to be too far
for the traveller of today who is in
a hurry? Spare an hour or two
for Dolanog – no stone cross,
no Holy Father. What question
has the country to ask, looking as if
nothing has happened since the earth
cooled? And what is your question?
She was young and was taken.
If one asked you : 'Are you glad
to have been born?' would you let
the positivist reply for you
by putting your car in gear, or watch
the exuberance of nature in a lost
village, that is life saying Amen
to itself? Here for a few years
the spirit sang on a bone bough
at eternity's window, the flesh trembling
at the splendour of a forgiveness
too impossible to believe in, yet believing.

Are the Amens over? Ann (Gymraeg)
you have gone now but left us with the question
that has a child's simplicity and a child's depth :
Does the one who called to you,

when the tree was green, call us
also, if with changed voice,
now the leaves have fallen and the boughs
are of plastic, to the same thing?

She listened to him.
We listen to her.
She was in time
chosen. We but infer
from the union of time
with space the possibility
of survival. She who was born
first must be overtaken
by our tomorrow.
So with wings pinned
and fuel rationed,

let us put on speed
to remain still
through the dark hours
in which prayer gathers .
on the brow like dew,
where at dawn the footprints
of one who invisibly
but so close passed
discover a direction.

Formula

And for the soul
in its bone tent, refrigerating
under the nuclear winter,
no epitaph prepared

in our benumbed language
other than the equation
hanging half-mast like the after-
birth of thought: $E = mc^2$.

Aubade

I awoke. There was dew,
and the voice of time singing:
It is too late to begin,
you are there already.

I went to the window
as to a peep-show: There she was
all fly-wheels and pistons;
her smile invisible

as a laser. And, 'No,'
I cried, 'No' turning away
into the computed darkness
where she was waiting

for me, with art's stone
rolled aside from her belly
to reveal the place poetry had lain
with the silicon angels in attendance.

Cones

Simple in your designs,
infinite in your variations
upon them: the leaf's veins,
the shell's helix, the stars themselves
gyring down to a point
in the mind; the mind also
from that same point spiralling
outward to take in space.

Heartening that in our journeys
through time we come round not
to the same place, but recognise it
from a distance. It is the dream
we remember, that makes us say:
'We have been here before.' In
truth we are as far from it
as one side of the cone
from the other, and in between
are the false starts, the failures,
the ruins from which we climbed,
not to look down, but to feel your glance
resting on us at the next angle
of the gyre.
           God, it is not your reflections
we seek, wonderful as they are
in the live fibre; it is the possibility
of your presence at the cone's
point towards which we soar
in hope to arrive at the still
centre, where love operates
on all those frequencies
that are set up by the spinning
of two minds, the one on the other.

Testimonies

The first stood up and testified to Christ:
I was made in the image of man; he unmanned me.

The second stood up: He appeared to me
in church in a stained window. I saw through him.

The third: Patient of love, I went
to him with my infirmity, and was not cured.

The fourth stood up, with between his thighs
a sword. 'He came not to bring peace' he said.

The fifth, child of his time, wasted his time
asking eternity: 'Who is my father and mother?'

So all twelve spoke, parodies of the disciples
on their way to those bone thrones from which they
        would judge others.

Coming

To be crucified
again ? To be made friends
with for his jeans and beard ?
Gods are not put to death

any more. Their lot now
is with the ignored.
I think he still comes
stealthily as of old,

invisible as a mutation,
an echo of what the light
said, when nobody
attended ; an impression

of eyes, quicker than
to be caught looking, but taken
on trust like flowers in the
dark country towards which we go.

The Fly

And the fly said: 'Nothing
to do. May as well
alight here.' No luck;
no poison. So man walked
immune down avenues
of vast promise, seeking
perfection. The fly
had it; filled in the time
flying, embroidering space
with the invisible meshwork
of flight's thread; spun rainbows
from light's spectrum. Man
worked more purposely
at his plans: immortality,
truth; killing the things would not
be killed, like time, love,
the one human, the other
one of the fly's ilk.
      What
is perfection? Anonymity's
patent? A frame fitted
for effortless success
in conveying viruses
to the curved nostril?
       I will not
be here long, but have seen
(among people) distorted
bodies, haloed with love,
shedding a radiance
where flies hung smaller
than the dust they say
man came from and to which,
I say, he will not return.

Apostrophe

Improvisers, he thinks,
making do with the gaps
in their knowledge; thousands of years
on the wrong track, consoling
themselves with the view by the way.
Their lives are an experiment
in deception; they increase
their lenses to keep a receding
future in sight. In arid
museums they deplore the sluggishness
of their ascent by a bone
ladder to where they took off
into space-time. They are orbited
about an unstable centre,
punishing their resources
to remain in flight.
                    There are no journeys,
I tell them. Love turns
on its own axis, as do beauty and truth,
and the wise are they
who in every generation
remain still to assess their nearness
to it by the magnitude of their shadow.

Fable

Winged life – why
respect it? A foretaste;
heaven dwellers? But look
what we do with what

we have – the smashed decibels,
the razed cities, all
to the ticking of the unhatched
egg in a Spartan temple.

Hebrews 12²⁹

If you had made it smaller
we would have fallen off; larger
and we would never have caught up
with our clocks. Just right
for us to know things are there
without seeing them? Forgive
us the contempt our lenses
breed in us. To be brought near
stars and microbes does us no good,
chrysalises all, that pupate
idle thoughts. We have stared and stared, and not stared
truth out, and your name has occurred
on and off with its accompanying
shadow. Who was it said: Fear
not, when fear is an ingredient
of our knowledge of you? The mistake
we make, looking deep into the fire,
is to confer features upon a presence
that is not human; to expect love
from a kiss whose only property is to consume.

Roles

How old was he, when he asked
who he was, and receiving
no answer, asked who they
were, who projected images
of themselves on an unwilling
audience. They named him, adding
the preliminary politeness, endorsing
a claim to gentility he did not
possess. The advance towards Christian
terms was to an understanding of the significance
of repentance, courtesy put under greater
constraint; an effort to sustain the role
they insisted that he had written.
Who reaches such straits flees
to the sanctuary of his mirror for re-assurance
that he is still there, challenging the eyes
to look back into his own and not
at the third person over his shoulder.

Gift

Some ask the world
  and are diminished
in the receiving
  of it. You gave me

only this small pool
  that the more I drink
from, the more overflows
  me with sourceless light.

Harvest End

(From the Welsh of Caledfryn)

The seasons fly;
the flowers wither;
the leaves lie
on the ground. Listen
to the sad song
of the reapers: 'Ripe
corn', as over the sea
the birds go.

Suddenly the year
ends. The wind rages;
everything in its path
breaks. Dire weather;
in front of a stick
fire, fetched from
the forest, firm and infirm
cower within doors.

The longest of lives
too soon slips by.
Careers fold and with
them good looks fade.
Spring's bloom is spent,
summer is done, too.
With a rush we come
to winter in the grave.

The Wood

A wood.
A man entered;
thought he knew the way
through. The old furies
attended. Did he emerge
in his right mind? The same
man? How many years
passed? Aeons? What is
the right mind? What does
'same' mean? No change of clothes
for the furies? Fast
as they are cut down
the trees grow, new
handles for axes.
There is a rumour from the heart
of the wood: brow
furrowed, mind
smooth, somebody huddles
in wide contemplation – Buddha,
Plato, Blake, Jung –
the name changes, identity
remains, pure being waiting
to be come at. Is it the self
that he mislaid? Is it why
he entered, ignoring
the warning of the labyrinth
without end? How many times
over must he begin again?

Biography

A life's trivia : commit them
not to the page, but to the waste-basket
of time. What was special
about you ? Did you write the great
poem ? Find the answer to the question :
When a little becomes much ?

You made war, campaigning upon the piano
that would surrender to the television.
Were you first in the race
for the cup of silver not to be drunk
from ? You ran fast and came home breathless
to the platitudes of the language.

Were you tall ? Taller than you
your best tales looked over your shoulder.
There was an apple tree with a girl
under it loitering as though
for you. It was not for you, but
she accepted you for want of a better.

Among scanty possessions fear
was yours. Courage you borrowed
on short loan ; set up house for the virtues
a wife brings. Venturing abroad
among the associated meannesses
you had all things in common.

Were you mobile ? So was the age ;
so were your standards, cheering
what yesterday was condemned
and tomorrow would be forgotten ;
turning left, when you should have gone right,
to prove determinism to be in error.

And one came to your back door
all bones and in rags, asking the kiss
that would have transformed both you
and him ; and you would not,
slamming it in his face, only
to find him waiting at your bed's side.

Zero

What time is it?
       Is it the hour when the servant
of Pharaoh's daughter went down
       and found the abandoned baby
in the bulrushes? The hour
       when Dido woke and knew Aeneas
gone from her? When Caesar
       looked at the entrails and took
their signal for the crossing
       of the dividing river?
                         Is it
that time when Aneirin
       fetched the poem out of his side
and laid it upon the year's altar
       for the appeasement of envious
gods?
       It is no time
at all. The shadow falls
       on the bright land and men
launder their minds in it, as
       they have done century by
century to prepare themselves for the crass deed.

The Bank

Meditating upon gold
we prick the heart on its thorns.

Yellow, yellow, yellow hair
of the spring, the poet cries,

admiring the gorse bushes
by the old stone wall. But the maiden's

hair overflows the arms
of the hero. Though you sit down

a thousand years, the echo
of the petals is inaudible

in the sunlight. Explain to me
why we use the same word

for the place that we store our money in,
and that other place where the gorse blows.

Revision

So the catechism begins:
'Who are you?'
                                    'I don't know.'
'Who gave you that ignorance?'
'It is the system that, when two people
meet, they combine to produce
the darkness in which the self
is born, a wick hungering
for its attendant flame.'
                                    'What will that
do for you?'
                                    'Do for me? It is the echo
of a promise I am meant
to believe in.'
                                    'Repeat that promise.'
'Whoever believes in this fire,
although he lives, he shall die.'
                                    'You
blaspheme. The promises were made
by you, not to you. What do you learn
from them?'
                                    'I learn there are two beings
so that, when one is present, the other
is far off. There is no room
for them both.'
                                    'Life's simpleton,
know this gulf you have created
can be crossed by prayer. Let me hear
if you can walk it.'
                                    'I have walked it.
It is called silence, and is a rope
                                    over an unfathomable
abyss, which goes on and on
never arriving.'

'So that your Amen
is unsaid. Know, friend, the arrival
is the grace given to maintain
your balance, the power which supplies
not the maggot of flame you desired,
that consumes the flesh, but the unseen
current between two points, coming
to song in the nerves, as in the telegraph
wires, the tighter that they are drawn.'

Similarities

I saw man staggering on his way
        with his un-necessaries. Where
was he going? He turned on me
those hurt eyes that are bold
in their weakness, bruised by a question
        he had not asked. Look,
he implied, sparing a glance
for the conjurors, the somersault
men, the mendicants with their caps brimming
        with dead leaves.
                              And
the mothers were there, nursing
a dead child, and the rich endowing
a mortuary. While the youth with hair
on his chest flaunted a tin
        cross.
                    Dance for me,
called the weak pipe, and the laughter
ascended to the rattle
        of a cracked drum.
                              My masters,
the machine whined, putting the yawning
consciences to sleep.
                          It is intolerable,
        I cried. But the face
that is life's trophy stared at me
from the gallery, where it had been set
        up, so that I became silent
before it, corrected by a resemblance.

AD 2000

The gyres revolve;
man comes to the confrontation
with his terror, with the imperative
of choice. Other compulsions are shown
for what they were. Time rinses its eyes
clean. From tyranny of the hand
we are delivered to the exigencies
of freedom, to the acknowledgement
by the unlimited of its limitations.

What power shall minister to us
at the closure of the century,
of the millennia? The god,
who was Janus-faced, is eclipsed
totally by our planet, by the shadow
cast on him by contemporary
mind. Shall we continue worshipping
that mind for its halo,
its light the mirage of its radiation?

Ritual

Not international
renown, but international
vocabulary, the macaronics
of time : μοῖρα, desiderium,
brad, la vida
breve, despair – I am the bone
on which all have beaten out
their message to the mind
that would soar. Faithful
in translation, its ploy was to evade
my resources. It saw
me dance through the Middle
Ages, and wrote its poetry
with quilled pen. What
so rich as the language
to which the priests
buried me? They have exchanged
their vestments for white coats,
working away in their bookless
laboratories, ministrants
in that ritual beyond words
which is the Last Sacrament of the species.

Calling

The telephone is the fruit
of the tree of the knowledge
of good and evil. We may call
everyone up on it but God.

To do that is to declare
that he is far off. Dialling
zero is nothing other
than the negation of his presence.

So many times I have raised
the receiver, listening to
that smooth sound that is technology's
purring; and the temptation

has come to experiment
with the code which would put
me through to the divine
snarl at the perimeter of such tameness.

Strands

It was never easy.
There was a part of us,
trailing uterine
memories, would have lapsed
back into Eden, the mindless
place. There was a part,
masochistic, terrifying itself
with a possibility – infinite
freedom in confrontation
with infinite love; the idea
of a balance, where we should come
to be weighed, lifting horrified
eyes to a face that was more
than human. And a part
amenable to the alternatives:
nature, mechanism, evolution,
bearers of a torch kindled
to illuminate primaeval
caves that has become electric,
the probing searchlight piercing
beyond the galaxies, shocking
the manipulator of it with its ability
to discover nothing, the ultimate
hole the intrepid reason
has dug for itself.
                  Must we
draw back? Is there a far side
to an abyss, and can our wings
take us there? Or is man's
meaning in the keeping of himself
afloat over seventy thousand
fathoms, tacking against winds
coming from no direction,
going in no direction?

Countering

Then there is the clock's
commentary, the continuing
prose that is the under-current
of all poetry. We listen
to it as, on a desert island,
men do to the subdued
music of their blood in a shell.

Then take my hand that is
of the bone the island
is made of, and looking at
me say what time it is
on love's face, for we have
no business here other than
to disprove certainties the clock knows.

April Song

Withdrawing from the present,
wandering a past that is alive
in books only. In love
with women, outlasted

by their smiles; the richness
of their apparel puts
the poor in perspective.
The brush dipped in blood

and the knife in art
have preserved their value.
Smouldering times: sacked
cities, incinerable hearts,

and the fledgling God
tipped out of his high
nest into the virgin's lap
by the incorrigible cuckoo.

The Window

Say he is any man
anywhere set before the shop window
of life, full of comestibles
and jewels; to put out his hand
is to come up against
glass; to break it is
to injure himself.
          Shall he turn
poet and acquire them
in the imagination, gospeller
and extol himself for his abstention
from them?
          What if he is not
called? I would put the manufacturers
there. Let them see the eyes
staring in, be splashed with the blood
of the shop-breakers; let them live
on the poet's diet, on the pocket-money
of the priest.
          I see the blinds
going down in Europe, over the
whole world: the rich with everything to
sell, the poor with nothing to buy it with.

Borders

Somewhere beyond time's
curve civilisation lifted
its glass rim. There was
a pretence of light

for nations to walk by
through the dark wood, where history
wintered. Following I came
to the foretold frontier

where with a machine's
instinct the guns' nostrils
flared at the blooms held out
to them by the flower people.

Retirement

I have crawled out at last
far as I dare on to a bough
of country that is suspended
between sky and sea.

From what was I escaping?
There is a rare peace here,
though the aeroplanes buzz me,
reminders of that abyss,

deeper than sea or sky, civilisation
could fall into. Strangers
advance, inching their way
out, so that the branch bends

further away from the scent
of the cloud blossom. Must
I console myself
with reflections? There are

times even the mirror
is misted as by one breathing
over my shoulder. Clinging
to my position, witnessing

the seasonal migrations,
I must try to content
myself with the perception
that love and truth have

no wings, but are resident
like me here, practising
their sub-song quietly in the face
of the bitterest of winters.

Questions

She should put off modesty
with her shift. Who said that?
Should one, then, put off belief
with one's collar? The girl enters
the bed, enters the man's
arms to be clasped between sheets
against the un-love that is all around.

The priest lies down alone
face to face with the darkness
that is the nothing from which nothing
comes. 'Love' he protests, 'love'
in spiritual copulation
with a non-body, hearing the echoes
dying away, languishing under the owl's curse.

What is a bed for? Is there no repose
in the small hours? No proofing of sleep's
stuff against the fretting of stars, thoughts?
Tell me, then, after the night's toil
of loving or praying, is there nothing
to do but to rise tired and be made
away with, yawning, into the day's dream?

Looking Glass

There is a game I play
with a mirror, approaching
it when I am not there,
as though to take by surprise

the self that is my familiar. It ·
is in vain. Like one eternally
in ambush, fast or slow
as I may raise my head, it raises

its own, catching me in the act,
disarming me by acquaintance,
looking full into my face as often
as I try looking at it askance.

The Cast

'Look up' they said
          at the rehearsal
of the film. 'Higher, higher' –
(preparing for the monster)
and the screaming began,
          the nightmare
from which there is no waking.
               Ah, vertical God,
whose altitudes are the mathematics
          that confound us,
what is thought but the mind's
          scream as it hurtles
in free-fall down your immense
side, hurrying everywhere,
arriving nowhere but at the precipitousness
          of your presence?
               We weigh

nothing. Is it that you assess
          us by our ability,
upside down as we are,
to look forward to averages
          that you have left behind?

Court Order

'My good fool' he
　　who was a king
said, 'come hither, perch
　　at my side; challenge
me to make some sport
　　with this word "Love".' I
did so, and was tumbled
　　into the world without
cap and bells, to end
　　up on a hard
shoulder, not laughing
　　with the rest who knew
that Friday, it being April,
　　was All Fools' Day.

Nativity

The moon is born
and a child is born,
lying among white clothes
as the moon among clouds.

They both shine, but
the light from the one
is abroad in the universe
as among broken glass.

Jerusalem

A city – its name
keeps it intact. Don't
touch it. Let the muezzin's
cry, the blood call

of the Christian, the wind
from sources desiccated
as the spirit drift over
its scorched walls. Time

devourer of its children
chokes here on the fact
it is in high places love
condescends to be put to death.

History

In the morning among colonnades
a Greek radiance. At mid-day
time stood vertically between them
and the answer that was not
far off. At mid-day somewhere else
time was appalled, seeing its shadow
dislocated by a body the issues
of which were for the conversion
of a soldier. Civilisation rounded
towards its afternoon, the languid siesta
of brawn and muscle. The monks' pupils
contracted through peering into
the reformed light. A vessel took off
into navigable waters to discover how mutinous
was the truth. As the sun went down
the lights came on in a million
laboratories, as the scientists attempted
to turn the heart's darkness into intellectual day.

A Thicket in Lleyn

I was no tree walking.
I was still. They ignored me,
the birds, the migrants
on their way south. They re-leafed
the trees, budding them
with their notes. They filtered through
the boughs like sunlight,
looked at me from three feet
off, their eyes blackberry bright,
not seeing me, not detaching me
from the withies, where I was
caged and they free.
                    They would have perched
on me, had I had nourishment
in my fissures. As it was,
they netted me in their shadows,
brushed me with sound, feathering the arrows
of their own bows, and were gone,
leaving me to reflect on the answer
to a question I had not asked.
'A repetition in time of the eternal
I AM.' Say it. Don't be shy.
Escape from your mortal cage
in thought. Your migrations will never
be over. Between two truths
there is only the mind to fly with.
Navigate by such stars as are not
leaves falling from life's
deciduous tree, but spray from the fountain
of the imagination, endlessly
replenishing itself out of its own waters.

Confrontation

And there was the serpent
running like water
but more quietly with no desire
to bicker. They see us
with smooth eye; what is man
in a snake's world? And if
we would come too close,
they strike us as painfully
as the truth.
                    It is no part
of divine mind to repudiate
its reflections. We must exchange
stare for stare, looking
into that eye as into a dark
crystal, asking if Eden
is where we must continually
seek to charm evil by playing
to it, knowing that it is deaf.

Moorland

It is beautiful and still;
        the air rarefied
as the interior of a cathedral

expecting a presence. It is where, also,
        the harrier occurs,
materialising from nothing, snow-

soft, but with claws of fire,
        quartering the bare earth
for the prey that escapes it;

hovering over the incipient
        scream, here a moment, then
not here, like my belief in God.

Unposted

Dear friend unknown,
why send me your poems?
We are brothers, I admit;
but they are no good.
I see why you wrote them,
but why send them? Why not
bury them, as a cat its faeces?
You confuse charity and art.
They have not equal claims,
though the absence of either
will smell more or less the same.

I use my imagination:
I see a cramped hand gripping
a bent pen, or, worse perhaps,
it was with your foot you wrote.
You wait in an iron bed
for my reply. My letter
could be the purse of gold
you pay your way with past
the giant, Despair.
                    I lower my standards
and let truth hit me squarely
between the eyes. 'These are great
poems,' I write, and see heaven's
slums with their rags flying,
cripples brandishing their crutches,
and the one, innocent of scansion,
who knows charity is short
and the poem for ever, suffering
my dark lie with all the blandness
with which the round moon suffers an eclipse.

Asking

Did I see religion,
its hand in the machine's,
trying to smile as the grip
tightened? Did I hear money

arguing out of the tree's
branches, shadowing
the world, about the love
at its root? How beautiful

in a world like this
are the feet of the peace
makers upon the mountains
risen out of our own molehills?

A Life

Lived long; much fear, less
courage. Bottom in love's school
of his class; time's reasons
too far back to be known.
Good on his knees, yielding,
vertical, to petty temptations.
A mouth thoughts escaped
from unfledged. Where two
were company, he the unwanted
third. A Narcissus tortured
by the whisperers behind
the mirror. Visionary only
in his perception of an horizon
beyond the horizon. Doubtful
of God, too pusillanimous
to deny him. Saving his face
in verse from the humiliations prose
inflicted on him. One of life's
conscientious objectors, conceding
nothing to the propaganda of death
but a compulsion to volunteer.

Folk Tale

Prayers like gravel
        Flung at the sky's
window, hoping to attract
        the loved one's
attention. But without
        visible plaits to let
down for the believer
        to climb up,
to what purpose open
        that far casement?
        I would
have refrained long since
        but that peering once
through my locked fingers
I thought that I detected
        the movement of a curtain.

Ystrad Fflur

(Strata Florida)

I hardly knew him.
The place was old,
ruins of an ideal in chaste
minds. Rows of graves
signalled their disappointment.
Time, I said. Place, he replied,
not contradicting.
                Had we found
what we sought, for him
somewhere, for me when
to listen to a mossed voice
beyond our dimensions?
Where are the twelve gates?
I wondered, looking at the low
archway through which we had come.
Had the years left us
only this one? Must masculine thoughts
once more be tonsured?
                  I am
a musician, the voice said.
I play on the bone keys in an audience's
absence. The light twitched,
as though at the blinking
of an immense eyelid; the foliage
rippled in shadowy applause.
We regarded one another,
neither wanting to be first
to propose. Is every proposal
a renunciation? Was our return
mutual to where the machine offered
its accelerating alternatives
to the noon-day of the soul?

Approaches

We began by being very close.
Moving nearer I found
he was further off, presence
being replaced by shadow;

the nearer the light, the larger
the shadow. Imagine the torment
of the discovery that it was growing
small. Is there a leak somewhere

in the mind that would comprehend
him? Not even to be able to say,
pointing: Here Godhead was spilled.
I had a belief once that even

a human being left his stain
in places where he had occurred.
Now it is all clinical light
pouring into the interstices

where mystery could linger
questioning credentials of the divine
fossil, sterilising our thought
for its launching into its own outer space.

Where?

Where to turn without turning
to stone? From the one side
history's Medusa stares,
from the other one love

on its cross. While the heart
fills not with light
from the mind, but with the shadow
too much of such light casts.

This One

Sometimes a shadow passed
between him and the light.
Sometimes a light showed itself
in the darkness beyond. Could
it be? The strong angels wrestled
and were not disposed to give
him the verdict. Are there journeys
without destinations? The animals
paused and became gargoyles
beside the way. And this one,
standing apart to confer
with the eternal, was he blamed
for reaction? There is always
laughter out of the speeding
vehicles for the man
who is still, half-way though he be
in a better direction. From receding
horizons he has withdrawn
his mind for greater repose
on an inner perspective,
where love is the bridge between
thought and time. Consumers
of distance at vast cost,
what do they know of the green
twig with which he divines,
where life balances excess
of death, the bottomless
water that is the soul's glass?

Truly

No, I was not born
to refute Hume, to write
the first poem with no
noun. My gift was

for evasion, taking
cover at the approach
of greatness, as of
ill-fame. I looked truth

in the eye, and was not
abashed at discovering
it squinted. I fasted
at import's table, so had

an appetite for the banal,
the twelve baskets full left
over after the turning
of the little into so much.

Retrospect

As they became
cleverer, they became worse –
So history publishes
its contempt for the scholars

who can't spell. One thing
I remember: There was
a man time should have
bowed down to: bones of a bird,

great brain, whose argument broke
on the big fist; while a girl wept
her confetti tears,
bellowing to be deflowered.

Andante

Masters, you who would initiate
me in discourse, apostrophising
the deity: O Thou, to Whom ...
out of date three hundred
years. The atoms translate
into their own terms, burnishing
the dust, converting it
to a presence, a movement of light
on the room's wall, a smile quickening
and going out as the clouds
canter. Inhabitants of a flower
they fix that gaze on us
which is without focus, but compels
the attention, mesmerising us until
we are adrift on its scent's timelessness.
The huskiness of an emotion!
Can molecules feel? There is the long sigh
from the shore, the wave clearing
its throat to address us, requiring
no answer than the due
we give these things that share
the world with us, that compose
the world: an ever-renewed
symphony to be listened to
admiringly, even as we perform
it on whatever instruments
the generations put into our hands.

A Country

It is nowhere,
          and I am familiar
with it as one is
with a song.
           I know its background,
              the terraces
of cloud that are the hanging gardens
             of the imagination.
No sun
          rises there, so there is no sun
to set. It is the mind
suffuses it with a light
          that is without
            shadows.
               Invisible fountains
play, though their skirts
are of silk.
          And who lives there,
you ask, who walks
its unmetalled highways?
          It is a people
who pay their taxes
          in poetry; who repair broken
names; who wear the past
as a button-hole at their children's
          marriage with what is to be.

Their Canvases Are

full of the timeless faces
of their kind, gazing out
at a distance that is empty
of our inventions and serene

so. The trees are dark
flames, burning in the Florentine
weather in answer to
the need of the blind hand

for form, kindling nothing
but the imagination, for
the earth that produced
these was fertile of

worse things: our shadows,
for instance. Fortunate
people, foreseeing so much
on the horizon, but never ourselves coming.

Aim

A voice out of the land –
animal, vegetable, mineral –
'The pain, the beauty – Why, why, why?
Tell me the truth, give me
understanding.'
     And the rose
wastes its syllables; the rock fixes
its stare; the stoat sips
at the brimmed rabbit.
     And one,
Ieuan Morgan, his mind
in a sling, goes on his way
past the crouched chapel,
its doors' barrels levelled
on him out of the last
century, neither knowing nor caring
whether he is a marked man.

Reply

Do the wheels praise,
         humming to themselves
as they proceed in unnecessary
         directions? Do the molecules
bow down? Before what cradle
         do the travellers from afar,
strontium and plutonium, hold out
         their thin gifts? What
is missing from the choruses
         of bolts and rivets, as they prepare
for the working of their expensive
         miracle high in the clerestories
of blind space? What anthem have our computers
         to insert into the vacuum caused
by the break in transmission
         of the song upon Patmos?

Cures

'We sat under a tree
at the season when elms
put forth their leaves. It was then
Guillemette Benet said to me:
"My poor friend, my poor friend,
the soul is nothing
but blood." '*

                  So the deposition
at Foix. Inquisitor,
what would you have the soul
be to escape the rigour
of your laundering? Your Christ
died for you; for whom
would you have these die?
No answer. He has withdrawn
iron-faced into the silence
from which history resurrects
everything but our reasons.

Meanwhile a few leagues
to the west, like a suppuration
of grace, the soiled fountain
plays, where the scientists gather
bacteria. Their claims are refuted
by the virgin smile on the face
of the water. Holy Church
has become wise, recognising
the anaemic soul is no substitute
for the bone's need.

                And the mind,
then, weary of the pilgrimages
to its horizons – is there no spring of thought
adjacent to it, where it can be
dipped, so that emerging but
once in ten thousand times,
freed of its crutches, is sufficient
testimony to the presence in it
of a power other than its own?

* From *Montaillou* by Emmanuel le Roy Ladurie, translated by Barbara Bray

Look Out

At the dance of the dust,
         at the recital
of flies, the master of ceremonies
is the scarecrow, brandishing
         his baton. Is this
evening-dress? we ask,
         admiring his shirt-front
of fresh straw.
            'Pouf' says the wind,
'by his lack of expression
         he conducts nothing,
not even himself.'
            'Are the crossed sticks
        where I must perch?' the dove
wonders.
        And history: 'I have wasted
           all my time
in ascending him, but
        there is no view from the top.'

Revision

Heaven affords
       unlimited accommodation
to the simple-minded.
             Pardon,
hymn-writers, if levity deputises
       for an Amen. Too much
has depended on the exigencies
       of rhyme. You never
improved on 'odd' as the antiphon
       to a heavenly father.
               Tell

me, is truth's victory followed
       by an armistice?
             How many
of man's prayers assume
       an eavesdropping God?
              A bishop

       called for an analysis
of the bread and wine. I being
       no chemist play my recording
of his silence over
       and over to myself only.

Fuel

And the machines say, laughing
up what would have been sleeves
in the old days: 'We are at
your service.' 'Take us', we cry,

'to the places that are far off
from yourselves.' And so they do
at a price that is the alloy in
the thought that we can do without them.

A Marriage

We met
    under a shower
of bird-notes.
    Fifty years passed,
love's moment
    in a world in
servitude to time.
    She was young;
I kissed with my eyes
    closed and opened
them on her wrinkles.
    'Come,' said death,
choosing her as his
    partner for
the last dance. And she,
    who in life
had done everything
    with a bird's grace,
opened her bill now
    for the shedding
of one sigh no
    heavier than a feather.

Index of Titles

Index of First Lines